CITY GOATS

CITY GOATS

THE GOAT JUSTICE LEAGUE'S GUIDE
TO BACKYARD GOAT KEEPING

JENNIE P. GRANT

PHOTOGRAPHY BY
HARLEY SOLTES

SKIPSTONE

Some of the names in this book have been changed to protect
the innocent and the guilty.

Published by Skipstone, an imprint of The Mountaineers Books
Printed in USA

First printing 2012
15 14 13 12   5 4 3 2 1

Copy Editor: Rebecca Pepper
Design: Jane Jeszeck, www.jigsawseattle.com
Cover photograph: Harley Soltes
Illustrator: Joshua McNichols
All photographs by Harley Soltes unless otherwise credited
Frontispiece: *When Melany Vorass has kitchen scraps, she opens her kitchen window and Lily reaches in,
devours the scrap, and turns it into a tidy pellet of compost gold within just twelve hours.*

Library of Congress Cataloging-in-Publication Data
Grant, Jennie Palches.
  City goats : the Goat Justice League's guide to backyard goat keeping
/ by Jennie Palches Grant ; photographs by Harley Soltes.
      p. cm.
  Includes index.
  ISBN 978-1-59485-699-0 (pbk) — ISBN 978-1-59485-700-3 (ebook)
  1. Goats. I. Title.
  SF383.G73 2012
  636.3'9—dc23
            2012019124

ISBN (paperback): 978-1-59485-699-0
ISBN (ebook): 978-1-59485-700-3

Skipstone
1001 SW Klickitat Way
Suite 201
Seattle, Washington 98134
206.223.6303
www.skipstonebooks.org
www.mountaineersbooks.org

SUSTAINABLE FORESTRY INITIATIVE
Label applies to the text stock
Certified Sourcing
www.sfiprogram.org
SFI-00341

LIVE LIFE. MAKE RIPPLES.

To my son,
Spencer Grant Kneass, for giving me
hope and encouragement
by finding parts of City Goats
entertaining, despite it containing
no real superheroes,
no disgusting but lovable aliens,
and no scary cliff-hangers

An attractive goat, goat shed, and well-tended goat yard can add visual interest to your garden.

CONTENTS

Eloise, who lives on a diet of blackberry leaves and alfalfa, wishes she could try a cupcake.

THOUGHTS REGARDING CITIFIED GOATS

THIS IS A BOOK ABOUT HOW TO CARE FOR URBAN DAIRY GOATS. You might think such a book is unnecessary, given that there are already plenty of goat-care books taking up space on bookshelves across America. You might even be thinking something like, "Do urban goats really need a book devoted to them? Deep down, isn't a goat just a goat, whether it lives in a hip and liberal urban center, a spacious farm run by survivalists, or a hippie alternative co-op in the country?" If you are thinking along these lines, you do have a point. Goats, whatever their socioeconomic status, whatever the style of their ears, whatever their stature, all have very similar needs. While their personalities do differ, what makes them happy, what feeds their souls and their rumens, is, at its innermost core, basically the same.

To conclude that a book on urban dairy goats is unnecessary, however, would be to conclude wrongly. Caring for an urban goat has unique challenges. Most urban ruminants don't have the land that their more fortunate country cousins enjoy. Some live in backyards as small as 400 square feet. These goats have neither dedicated kidding stalls nor barns full to the rafters with alfalfa from the field out back.

In many ways, the special needs of the urban goat can be compared with the special needs of your average Manhattanite. For example, in Manhattan, due to the prohibitive cost of real estate, apartments must be ingeniously designed to ensure that every square inch serves a purpose. In much the same way, urban goats require cleverly designed goat sheds that can serve as shelter in a storm, kidding stall, and kid pen.

In addition, because so much of the natural world of Manhattan has been torn down and replaced with skyscrapers, there is little left in the way of natural beauty to enrich the lives of Manhattan's inhabitants. As a result, Manhattanites are constantly in the market for interesting toys and engaging activities. This is how Broadway came to be. Ditto 5th Avenue. Just like Manhattanites, urban goats require entertainment in lieu of bounteous natural surroundings. They require special goat playscapes, feeders that provide brush in the shape of a bush, and occasional human companionship and interaction.

Exercise is another problem for the residents of New York, and even for residents of the suburbs and rural outlands. Modern Americans, unlike the farmers of old, who did physical labor from sunup to sundown, do not get the exercise they need while going about their daily business. As a result, they must join health clubs and walk or run for the sole purpose of walking or running. Such is the case with city goats. Without acres to roam in search of their daily bread, urban goats do best if they get a half hour of cardio work every day.

Although this book will stress the special needs of urban goats, it will also focus on the needs of the inexperienced urban goat keeper. Many of the goat care books on the market today can leave someone just embarking on the adventure of goat keeping with the feeling that he or she must be able to head out to the goat shed with a .22 to cull the herd, own and know how to use an emasculator to neuter young bucklings, and take a red hot disbudding iron to the head of a four-day-old kid to prevent horns from growing. This book aims to remind you that you do not need the heart and muscle of a Civil War surgeon to own goats. There is no shame in writing a check to have these unpleasant tasks done for you. In fact, for those with small herds of two or three goats, hiring a skilled professional is often more economical than purchasing the tools to do the tasks yourself.

My experience with keeping goats has brought me much joy, and I have learned a great deal—not just about goats, but about people as well. From the questions friends ask me, such as, "You mean goats don't just spontaneously lactate? They have to have kids first?" I have discovered how wildly out of touch we all are with our food. And from haggling with city officials over what constitutes a pet vs. a farm animal, I have come to think critically of our culture's insistence upon distinguishing between the two. Despite being a nation of animal lovers, where many dogs are so well fed that they require diet kibble, a majority of the states in our nation, particularly the agricultural ones, exempt farm animals from animal cruelty laws. Goats have helped me see how very wrong and problematic this distinction really is.

Goat keeping is certainly not for everyone. In fact, it probably makes sense for only a tiny percentage of people. However, goats in the cities and suburbs, when well cared for, bring not just fresh milk, but perhaps also fresh thought—about milk quality, factory-farmed animals, animal ethics, vegetarianism and veganism, the human-animal connection, and community. Initially, the idea of city goats strikes most people as absurd, but in fact it makes sense. My hope is that, by the time you finish reading this book, if someone says to you "urban goats," your odd visions of glamorous city goats heading to the opera will be replaced by a sense that goats belong wherever capable and dedicated goat enthusiasts reside.

—Jennie P. Grant, Founder and President, Goat Justice League

Maple stands tall on top of her hay storage box in the goat yard.

CHAPTER ONE

DO GOATS BELONG IN YOUR BACKYARD?

WHILE IT IS TRUE THAT NO SENSIBLE PERSON would move from the country to the city to keep goats, should a city person who wants to keep goats have to move to the country? I say no, and that is where city goats come in. A conscientious owner can keep a pair of goats healthy and happy within a 400-square-foot area (though more is better) if he or she is willing to put in the time, effort, and money. He or she will need to construct a very cleverly designed goat shed that makes careful use of space. In addition, to keep a goat healthy, city dwellers will need to go out foraging to bring home fresh greens for their goats. A goat can live on good-quality hay and alfalfa pellets but cannot thrive without plenty of fresh greens.

But who would want to keep goats in the first place? Given that you are reading this book, I'm guessing that you are considering the idea and are wondering, "Should I go through with this?" This is a good question, because some people are interested in goats for the wrong reasons. To find out if you may be trotting down the wrong goat path, here are some questions to ask yourself:

Do you want to keep goats so that you will never have to mow your lawn?

If so, think again. Goats will eat your rosebushes clean, carefully devouring every single leaf and flower. However, they are not going to mow your lawn. They will nibble at grass here and there in a sort of unorganized fashion, creating a look very similar to Rod Stewart's hairstyle.

Have you been thinking of getting a pair of goats to clear the brush that has taken over your yard?

If so, goats will disappoint. Since you've probably read the news stories about goats clearing hillsides of invasive nonnatives, you should know that goats don't do this work without human help. It's true that goats are extremely efficient at nibbling blackberry leaves, but they won't eat the canes unless they are starving. The brush-clearing services have people who follow behind the goats and clear out the deleafed branches and haul them away. Why do the media ignore these people and focus just on the goats, thereby getting the story wrong every single time? It is because people and goats clearing land together are just not nearly as entertaining as goats doing it alone. This is not to say that goats will not help you clear brush. They will, but their help will only go so far. If your problem is blackberries, they'll defoliate the branches within their reach, but you'll need to cut and haul away the defoliated bramble so they can eat their way through your thicket.

Are you looking to connect more with nature?

If so, here are some things to consider. Goats will help connect you with nature simply by getting you outside. This can be good and bad. For example, you may wake up one winter morning to hear wind swooshing about the trees, rain drumming against your roof, and white water pounding out your downspouts as you lie in bed warm and drowsy. You might be thinking how nice it would be to stay inside all day. Goats will not allow such behavior. They will force you out to haul hay, empty buckets, and attend to their milking. You will brace yourself as you step outside on such a morning, but you'll soon warm up and perhaps even enjoy being out in the storm.

Are you looking for a more relaxed lifestyle?

Goats require a minimum of 40 minutes of work per day, and this work is unrelenting. If you milk twice a day, you must milk every single morning and every single evening for the full period during which they are in milk (about nine months of the year). This aspect of goat keeping does have an upside. You can give yourself a break by recruiting backup milkers who will help you with milking a time or two a week in exchange for milk. Locating and training these backup milkers can be difficult, but getting to know people who are interested in your goats and sharing your knowledge can be rewarding.

How do you feel about exercise?

Keeping goats is physically demanding. Goats eat a tremendous volume of food and you will often find yourself faced with the job of hauling several 50-pound bags of alfalfa pellets or bales of hay out to your goat yard. And you may find yourself cursing as you wrestle with your goat in an effort to trim her hooves. All this requires strength and determination and may not be your cup of tea. On the upside, such activity is more exciting than that hamster wheel of a StairMaster.

Are you so into gardening that you've considered sneaking into your neighbors' yard in the middle of the night to steal some of their compost?

If so, a goat may be for you. Goat poop is an even better soil amendment than rabbit droppings and can be added directly to the soil without composting (but if you'll be using it for food crops, the Seattle Health Department recommends composting it for a year). Goats are like miracle compost machines. They can turn your weeds into valuable compost within twenty-four hours. What's more, they can do what few compost systems can—kill the seeds of even the most virile weeds. Unlike horse manure, goat manure can be spread on your garden without the worry that it will seed a new crop of dandelions.

Are you nuts about animals and not already feeling overwhelmed by too many?

Many people who are allergic to dogs are not allergic to goats. Like dogs, goats are friendly and curious animals. When you step into their goat yard, they may greet you with a nuzzle. They may nibble at your clothing. And when it comes time for your goat to give birth, you'll quite literally get to witness the miracle of life. There is nothing like watching two kids plop out of their mother and onto your goat shed floor. As you watch the new mother dedicatedly licking her kids clean and gently bleating to them, you will marvel at the wonders of the animal world. And as you watch the kids take their first few steps and lunge awkwardly in search of a milk-laden teat, you will consider packing it all up and moving to the country to buy even more goats.

Do you like the adventure of meeting new people with lifestyles different from your own?

Discover the interesting realm of the goat enthusiast! Having goats will draw you out to feed stores where they sell Carhartt clothing, baby chicks, fabulous muck boots, and bales of hay in a whole array of varieties you never even knew existed. You will search for blackberry bushes in alleys around your neighborhood that you've never ventured down before. You will head to country fairs, where you won't be able to stop yourself from asking people with goats about the benefits of alfalfa over orchard grass. You may even one day find yourself down a long dirt road on the grounds of a faraway farm, face to face with a smelly and lascivious stud buck. In short, having goats will broaden your world.

Have you got room in your life for more friends?

You'd be surprised how goats can fill up your social calendar. Once you have goats, you will inevitably meet other goat keepers. You will get to talking about the type of concentrate you feed your goat, and why you chose it and how much you feed, and they will tell you about what they consider to be the finest spot in their neighborhood for collecting blackberry leaves. You may have spirited debates over what is more important, the size of the teat, the ability to let down, or the size and tightness of the orifice of the teat. Whatever subject you hit upon, you will probably enjoy yourself and find you've made new friends.

Are you looking for an inexpensive source of milk?

If so, do not get dairy goats. When you take into account the cost of housing, feed, and medical care, you would do far better buying your milk at the grocery store. It costs about $75 a month to feed a pair of goats.

Lastly, if you care deeply about the quality of the milk you drink, and you hate the idea of buying milk from a factory farm, goat keeping may be for you.

While milk from your backyard goats will be expensive when compared with the milk from Safeway, it will be of an exceptional quality, unlike any found in a supermarket. The topic of milk has many facets, and if you are interested in keeping dairy goats for milk, there's a great deal to know.

If after reading all this, you are still excited about the prospect of getting goats, this book is for you. I've written this book with the newbie suburban/urban goat owner in mind. I'll go over the basics of what to feed your goats and how to train them on the milking stand and share with you some of the interesting experiences I've encountered in my efforts to legalize and raise goats in my city of Seattle.

Eloise greets
visitors at the gate
to her goat yard.

Snowflake looks out at Lake Washington and thinks about chewing her cud.

CHAPTER TWO

WHAT YOU SHOULD KNOW ABOUT GOAT MILK

AFTER BECOMING ENAMORED OF GOATS, I decided to look into the health benefits of goat milk. I wanted to find out whether goat milk was superior to cow milk and how the milk from goats given sunshine and the right food compared with that of factory-farmed goat milk. But what popped up in all of my initial searches surprised me: Milk, it seems, is a polarizing food. There are websites galore devoted to promoting milk and websites galore devoted to demonizing it. Some people believe it is a nutritional nightmare and argue that it is the root cause of arthritis, anemia, and stomach pain. Others argue that it is the perfect food. What's an average person who doesn't have a PhD in the biology of nutrition to think?

How Milk Made Enemies

In the late 1700s, Europeans began to think of fresh, unfermented milk as the perfect food. Why they began to think this is not clear, but it may have been due to the fact that fresh milk was extremely perishable. My theory is that, like morning dew, fresh milk was so fleeting that it was thought of as special and so took on the reputation of a superfood.

Whatever the reason, people believed that fresh milk was extremely healthful, especially for children. Over time, this belief became so ingrained that when lactose intolerance was discovered in the 1960s, few people took notice. The ideas that milk is (1) not needed in the diet and (2) more easily digested if fermented first struck the public and medical professionals as nutritional blasphemy. Despite breakthroughs in research indicating that milk is not necessary in the human diet and could be harmful, doctors, the federal government's school lunch programs, and nutritionists alike have continued to promote it as a perfect and indispensable food.

Yet milk, especially unfermented milk, is not the perfect food and never has been. Furthermore, there's milk and then there's milk. There is a huge difference between modern factory-farmed milk that is ultrapasteurized and homogenized and has a shelf life of six months and milk from animals that get sunshine, exercise, and lots of fresh greens to eat. They are both called milk, but they are not the same thing.

Not being perfect wouldn't make milk a target if lots of people hadn't touted it for hundreds of years as the perfect food. Nobody likes a braggart, especially one with little to brag about. My theory is that milk, while a perfectly good food, is the victim of its own overly enthusiastic boosters. I remember being taught in grade school that you could tell that milk was the perfect food just by looking at babies. Babies drank only milk for the first six months of their lives, and they thrived. Milk, it was reasoned, had absolutely everything in it a person needed to live. When word got out that the enzymes necessary to digest lactose fade from most mammals' digestive systems at the age of weaning, some people (probably those who didn't like drinking milk in the first place) became annoyed with the milk boosters and took careful aim.

FACTORY FARMING CHANGED MILK

The milk that most Americans drink today is cow milk, but it is far different from the cow milk of yesteryear. The modern cow produces significantly more milk than her predecessors. Between 1960 and today, the amount of milk the average cow produces in a year has tripled. This increase has been caused by three factors: the feeding of large quantities of grain, the use of bovine growth hormones (BGH or rBST), and both artificial insemination and embryo transfer (technologies that allow cows and bulls known to have excellent genetics to reproduce like rabbits).

This phenomenal growth in milk production has come at a high cost. In 1950, farmers kept their cows for an average of fourteen years. Today, most dairy cows are culled at five years of age. And what of the quality of the milk produced by these supercows? It is a pale and watered-down version of its former self.

In 1929, the best herds produced milk containing 5 or even 5.5 percent milk fat (Mendelson). Today, the standard is considered to be 3.25 percent. In addition, the milk fat produced by the modern factory-farmed cow is markedly different from that of a cow raised on pasture and fed little or no concentrate. A study reported in the *Journal of Dairy Science* found that the milk of cows fed purely on pasture contained five times as much conjugated linoleic acid (CLA) as the milk of cows fed the typical factory diet of 50 percent silage and 50 percent grain (Dhiman et al.). CLA is now thought by many researchers to be the most effective essential fatty acid in preventing and slowing cancer. Certain types of CLA have also been shown to prevent cardiovascular disease. My personal favorite CLA discovery is that it increases belly firmness in pigs (Eggert et al.).

Milk from pasture-fed cows also contains a better ratio of omega-3s to omega-6s. Recent research has found that foods with equal amounts of omega-3s and omega-6s have the ability to improve your health in almost every way. They can lower your risk of cancer, cardiovascular disease, autoimmune disorders, allergies, obesity, and diabetes, as well as dementia and various other mental disorders (Simopoulos and Robinson). Milk from cows fed purely on pasture has this miraculous 1-to-1 ratio. By contrast, the milk of your average factory-farmed cow has an omega-3 to omega-6 ratio of 1 to 5—not a healthy balance.

Because the market for goat milk is tiny compared to the market for cow milk, little research has been done on how the quality of milk from woodland-raised goats compares with that of factory-farmed goat milk. Michael Pollan put forth a theory in his book *The Omnivore's Dilemma* that food raised in consideration of what is best for the animals, best for the workers, and best for the environment is also bound to be more nutritious. If this theory holds true for goat milk, then the milk from goats that eat a large amount of leaves should be more nutritious than the milk of factory-farmed goats that eat mostly silage and grain.

LACTOSE INTOLERANCE AND FERMENTED MILK

Before mammals are weaned, they produce an enzyme called lactase that enables the easy digestion of milk sugar (lactose). Once a mammal passes the age of weaning, it slowly loses, to some degree, its ability to produce lactase and thus its ability to digest lactose. Given that humans are mammals, this is true for your average human as well. When a person who can produce only small amounts of lactase drinks a cup or two of unfermented milk, he or she will suffer some amount of stomach cramps, nausea, bloating, acid reflux, or flatulence. This is called lactose intolerance, a condition common to approximately 75 percent of the world's population.

While only 2 percent of people of northern European descent are lactose intolerant (they don't lose the ability to produce lactase), other ethnic groups suffer lactose intolerance at far greater rates—100 percent of indigenous Americans, 95 percent of Asians, and 50–80 percent of Hispanics.

You may hear it said that historically dairy products were commonly consumed only in Europe. This is untrue. Consumption of dairy products was just as prevalent in Africa and India as it was in Europe. However, it is also true that in most of the world, and in Europe until the 1700s, most milk was fermented before it was consumed. This made sense given the lack of refrigeration, as fermented milk lasts longer. It also made sense because fermenting milk causes a dramatic decrease in lactose content. Thus, lactose-intolerant people can consume fermented milk drinks and cheese with relative ease.

In It for the Milk? What You Can Expect

The quality and amount of milk you can expect your goat to give depends on the type of breed she is, her general health and ancestry, how many kids she gives birth to, and what and how much you feed her.

GOAT MILK VS. COW MILK

Some people prefer goat milk over cow milk. If you ask them, most goat-milk drinkers will tell you that it sits better with their stomachs. Since goat milk contains only slightly less lactose than cow milk (10 percent less), the reason for this may be that goat milk contains different proteins, and some people can digest these proteins more easily than the proteins in cow milk.

While people will point to the differing proteins and fats in goat milk as good reasons to consume it, few people will tell you that they choose goat milk because of the taste. Until I was in my early forties, I believed that goat milk was horrible tasting, and when I heard that more people in the world drink goat milk than drink cow milk, I felt sorry for that goat milk–drinking majority. I have since learned that what I hated was *grocery store* goat milk. Grocery store goat milk has a taste quite similar to the smell of a buck in rut. It has a gamy, earthy flavor that is good in a cheese but not so good with a bowl of cereal or a cup of coffee. When I first tasted very fresh goat milk—milk that I had helped milk from the goat, I was shocked. It was indistinguishable from cow milk, except perhaps for being richer. It turns out that goat milk, due to the presence of short-chain fatty acids, is much more fragile than cow milk, and it takes on the goaty taste only after a week in the refrigerator or if it is handled roughly. Milk that has made it to the shelves of a typical grocery store has undergone lots of piping, transporting, processing, and distributing. Thus, finding fresh, non-goaty-tasting goat milk at a typical large-scale grocery store, or even at a small food co-op, is difficult.

The taste of goat milk also depends on the breed of goat. Some breeds, such as Toggenburg, are said to produce milk with a gamier taste. Apparently, the people raising Toggenburgs were very interested in making a nice, tangy goat cheese, and so they bred for a nice, tangy milk. I have also heard that the higher the fat content of goat milk, the longer it can stay clean tasting, and Toggenburgs produce milk with a relatively low milk-fat content.

There are a few claims about off-tasting goat milk that are probably rural myth. One is that the presence of bucks on a farm causes the milk to taste bad, an idea that may have developed because the off taste is so reminiscent of the smell that rutty bucks give off. However, I have tasted fresh milk from goats on farms with bucks present, and it tastes just as sweet and clean as the milk from my goats. Another claim is that the tangy taste of some goat milk is due to the feed. But I've never noticed a change in the taste of my goats' milk when I've altered their feed. True, I've never fed them onions or asparagus, but I have fed them blackberry bramble, which some books will tell you can lead to foul-tasting milk. From my experience, off-tasting goat milk comes primarily from letting the milk sit in the refrigerator for more than a week.

HOW MUCH MILK DOES A MILK GOAT GIVE WHEN A MILK GOAT DOES GIVE MILK?

The question of how much milk you can expect is further complicated by the lactation curve. The amount of milk a goat gives varies considerably throughout the year. For example, when you begin milking, you will probably get just a few cups each morning, but slowly, day by day, the amount of milk you get per milking will increase. Between eight and twelve weeks after kidding, your goat will reach her lactation peak, and from that time on, the amount of milk she produces will slowly decline. Some goats will completely dry out during the winter. Others will continue giving milk into the spring, and then, as the days grow longer, will increase their milk production. However, in their second year of lactation, even the best goats will give only about 75 percent of what they gave during their first year. The ability to continue producing milk throughout the year of kidding and beyond is called lactation duration. A goat that can give milk for a full two years after kidding is said to have excellent lactation duration.

When considering what type of goat to get, it's important to look not just at how much milk the goat can produce at her peak, but also at the duration of her lactation. The table in Chapter 4 illustrates how many cups of milk per day goats of different breeds produce. As a general rule, mini-versions of goats produce approximately 75 percent of what a full-sized goat would produce. Some goats are outstanding producers for their breed, while others are subpar. Thus, although your average La Mancha will give more milk than your average Oberhasli, some Oberhaslis will produce more than some La Manchas. In addition, some mini-goats can outperform a standard version of their breed.

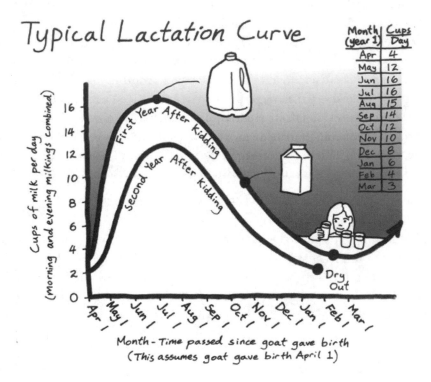

Typical Lactation Curve

Month (year 1)	Cups Day
Apr	4
May	12
Jun	16
Jul	16
Aug	15
Sep	14
Oct	12
Nov	10
Dec	8
Jan	6
Feb	4
Mar	3

Cups of milk per day (morning and evening milkings combined)

First Year After Kidding

Second Year After Kidding

Dry Out

Month - Time passed since goat gave birth
(This assumes goat gave birth April 1)

Milk production is influenced by the time of year and by the amount of time passed since kidding.

Eloise nibbles alfalfa from a metal hay manger.

A pause during Eloise's daily constitutional

LEGALIZING GOATS IN THE CITY

PEOPLE OFTEN ASK ME, "WHAT MADE YOU DECIDE to get goats?" or "Oh, you grew up in the country, eh?" The truth is, I often wonder this myself. I grew up in the suburbs, far from goats, and I have no idea why goat keeping has such great appeal to me. What I do know is that, for whatever reason, the idea of a backyard animal has been with me since childhood.

When I was young, in the 1960s, redlining (banks denying mortgages to nonwhites in certain neighborhoods) was common in our part of California, and my parents offered the mother-in-law apartment in our basement to a couple who needed a place to stay while trying to buy and finance a home. My mother was surprised when the couple arrived at our doorstep. The husband was 6 foot 3, had been educated at the Sorbonne, dressed impeccably, drove a Jaguar, and spoke with a lyrical African accent. His name was Mama Du Djay, and he was a pilot for Tiger Airlines. One day, before flying to Senegal, he asked if I'd like anything from Africa. I told him that as a matter of fact, I had been wanting an elephant for some time. "But where would you keep it?" he asked. "In the backyard," I answered.

He mentioned some concerns about weight limits and airplanes, flew off to Africa, and returned with a beautifully carved ebony elephant. I was disappointed. Had I not made myself clear? I wanted a *live* elephant.

I also remember taking trips to Angel Island, a lovely island park in the San Francisco Bay. During the 1970s, the deer population there exploded, and the deer ate every bit of vegetation within deer height. Eventually, the deer became so hungry that they'd come right up to you and eat pretzels out of your hand. You could see their ribs. I felt strongly that the right thing to do would be to bring them home to live in our backyard, and then, whenever I wanted, I could visit with them and feed them pretzels. As far as I was concerned, this was a win-win solution. Sadly, my parents and the parks department did not agree.

I Meet Dairy Goats Face-to-Face

As I got older, I forgot my dreams of elephants and deer in the backyard. I adopted two pug dogs and was content. But then one day I got the idea of having a flock of laying hens. Soon I was collecting eggs every morning. Some people jokingly refer to chickens as a "gateway farm animal," which just goes to show that much truth is said in jest. The chickens got me hooked on the idea of farm-fresh food from the backyard. Soon I wanted more, and in reading about the conditions of modern milk cow dairies, I began to wish for a cow—a tiny one. When I mentioned this whimsy to a friend, she said, "Why not get a goat?" "Because goat milk tastes terrible," I said, for at that time, store-bought goat milk was all I knew.

I thought nothing more about elephants, deer, cows, or goats in the backyard until a couple of years later, while visiting my cousin Monte Christie (that really is his name) in California. His co-worker, Abigail, had goats, and she invited me and my five-year-old son over to her place to meet her goats and watch her milk. We jumped at the chance, and I was immediately besotted. I cannot say why I loved the goats and the milking, but I did. I remember wondering, as I still wonder today, how it is that, given the amount of milk and cheese I consume, I'd never had an opportunity to milk an animal before.

Although I was thrilled to try milking, I was not thrilled to try the milk. When offered a taste, I politely declined, explaining that I'd tried goat milk and did not like it. Abigail pressed, I gave in, and much to my surprise, I liked it. It tasted sweet and smooth and creamy and would work very nicely on my morning oatmeal. Perhaps a goat would be my tiny backyard cow.

We had bought a new house only a few months before this visit, and in the backyard was a 20-by-20-foot patch of land, down behind a 10-foot retaining wall, that we'd been clearing of laurel bushes, ivy, and blackberry. The small plot was a good distance from the house, had no access by stair, and was shady and dark. To get to it, you needed to bring out a ladder and climb down. We'd come to call it the "back forty." It abutted a vacant lot, was well hidden from the street, and was a good distance from any neighboring houses. We had tried to think of what to do with it, but hadn't come up with anything.

I called my husband the evening of my first California goat-milking experience and told him enthusiastically that I had a great idea for the back forty. "Goats!"

"No goats," he said.

He had many reasons why he thought goats were a bad idea. They would be attacked by neighborhood dogs. Conversely, they would attack children. They would smell horrible. They would be despised by neighbors. They would give poor-tasting milk. They were illegal. I brushed aside these concerns. Abigail's goats did not smell. Dogs could not get into our yard. Goats did not generally attack. There was the issue of their being illegal, but perhaps no one would notice them. I could not shake the idea, and after many animated discussions, my husband at last sank his head into his hands and said, "Okay, if you must, but it is *not* a good idea."

Now I just needed to find the right goats. I began my search on the Internet, looking for "mini-goats" in the Seattle region, and lucked upon glimmercroft.com, a farm just 45 minutes north. When I went to visit the herd and saw the young doeling that was for sale standing on a hillock in her goat yard chewing her cud and gazing out at the horizon in a peaceable sort of way, I was hooked. I went home and finished clearing the back forty, built a goat shed, installed a fence, and a few months later brought home two goats, Snowflake and Brownie.

For the next eight months, my goat keeping proceeded without a hitch. Snowflake and Brownie did not attack any children, did not break out and jump on any neighboring Mercedes, and did not get attacked by dogs. They didn't smell, and they were, with a few exceptions, quiet. So the day that things went terribly wrong with my goat keeping was a big surprise.

Snowflake and Brownie Are Outed, or How My Illegal Activities Were Discovered

Sadly, a little girl a quarter-mile from our home came down with a mysterious illness that turned into another illness that was life-threatening. Preliminary tests indicated she might have Q fever, a disease carried by goats. When the girl's doctors asked her parents if there were goats in their neighborhood, they exclaimed, "Why yes. We've heard there is a woman in our neighborhood with goats." With their daughter deathly ill of an unexplained disease, they grasped at the Q fever straw and began to tell people that my goats were spreading a life-threatening disease. I could understand their anxiety, but given that the girl had never been to my home, let alone touched my goats, it seemed unlikely that Snowflake and Brownie had anything to do with her sickness. I invited the health department's veterinary epidemiologist to come and see the goats and where they were kept. She felt that they were well quarantined and that it would be highly unlikely for them to spread disease. In addition, I had my goats tested and found they had never been exposed to Q fever. Within a few weeks, additional tests on the girl showed that she probably had cat scratch fever contracted from the family's own cat. But by that time the damage was done. I had been reported to the Department of Planning and Development. Although concerns about my goats died down, the issue was now in the hands of the DPD, and the DPD insisted that my goats were farm animals and that their remaining in my yard was a violation of the zoning code.

Unsure of what to do, I wrote to Richard Conlin, a Seattle city council member who lived in my neighborhood and who I had read was working on local food and food security issues. His legislative aide, Phyllis Schulman, contacted me right away and came to my home to meet Snowflake and Brownie and see my goat yard setup. Initially, I asked if she might be able to help me get a waiver for my goats, but she explained that such waivers didn't exist. She liked the idea of goats in the city and said, "Let's see if we can't just get the law changed."

Richard Conlin, President of the Seattle City Council at left; Jill Lewis (owner of Richard Conlin the Kid); and Richard Conlin the Kid (aka Little Richard)

Was this even possible? Phyllis thought yes, why not? My goats were quiet and well behaved and, unlike cats, didn't wander freely and treat other people's vegetable gardens as their personal kitty litter boxes. (Apparently, she had a neighbor cat that was always pooping in her carrot patch, and this really made her mad.) Besides, Phyllis thought there might be other people in Seattle who would like to keep goats.

The idea that a city councilmember's staff would be willing to help me change the law astonished and delighted me.

Phyllis Schulman and namesake Phyllis Schulman the Kid

Phyllis asked if I would be willing to gather community support if she took care of the administrative details. I was, and with that we shook hands.

Phyllis went right to work. She gained the support of the health department and investigated what other cities allowed goats and whether said goats ever caused problems. She spoke with Seattle's animal control department to find out if they had the ability to catch and care for lost goats. In addition to this extensive research, Phyllis began filing the necessary notices for code change and convening the necessary meetings. And when the meetings took place, Phyllis was there with a whole spread of goat cheese.

I'm Pro-Goat and I Vote!

In the meantime, I set out to gather signatures. I first took my petition across the street to the Farmers' house, and as Mrs. Farmer gave me her John Hancock, I realized that my petition was missing something. I needed an official name, so that I could say I was collecting signatures for an actual organization. I decided I'd call my organization the Association for the Legalization of Mini-Dairy Goats, aka the Goat Justice League. In the beginning, I couldn't decide between the two names, hence the "aka." Many people assume that the Goat Justice League was inspired by the Superhero Justice League, but it wasn't. I had been thinking about the League of Women Voters—a group I have always admired for its moderate, sensible, and educated approach to politics. "Justice" I added because it communicated fairness but had an air of pompousness about it, too. I found out early on that the Goat Justice League was the superior name when a friend of mine came back from her rowing club with a sheet full of signatures and said, "There's this very conservative middle-aged lawyer on the team. When I gave him the petition, he looked at it begrudgingly and then, while signing it, mumbled, 'I never sign petitions, but what is this Goat Justice League? How can I not support them?'"

To get signatures, I sent petitions home with friends, and when they brought them back full, I repaid the favor in goat cheese. This got me several hundred signatures. The real bonanza, which took me to one thousand signatures, was the Seattle Tilth Harvest Fair—a celebration of organic gardening. This fair is always packed with organic farmers selling their produce, a few good bands, and demonstrations of poultry raising and bee keeping. Tilth allowed me to bring Snowflake and Brownie, and with those two beside me, and several friends armed with clipboards helping me work the crowd, we were able to gather a signature every three minutes.

It was at the Harvest Fair that we also rolled out our membership opportunity, which turned out to be a hit with the public. Just before the Harvest Fair, a journalist asked me about the number of members in my organization, and I realized that I didn't actually have any. I figured that to get card-carrying members, I'd first need some cards. Then, I'd just need to convince people to carry them. At the fair, after someone agreed to sign the petition, I'd follow up by asking if they'd like to be a card-carrying member. They'd often look at me sort of funny, and you could tell they were thinking that I was going to hit them up for money, so I'd quickly explain that there was no cost. They'd just need to take the card and carry it around sometimes. I had a hundred card-carrying Goat Justice League members in a single afternoon. I could have gotten even more, but I ran out of cards. The cards were especially popular among twenty-somethings. Word about the cards got out at the fair, and young people would come up and ask for them. They all said things like, "This is going to be great at a party." (This got me wondering about the state of twenty-something parties these days.)

Although I was sorely tempted to seek out the media to discuss the issue of goat legalization, Phyllis Schulman warned me not to. "The media is fickle," she explained. "You never know if it will fry you or sing your praises." She advised me to sit still and wait for the media to contact me. Phyllis also suggested that I frame the issue as one of tolerance rather than of opting out of the larger food system. I took Phyllis's advice and let the media find the story on its own. When they did call, I'd say, "I just love going out in the morning to milk my goats, and I like to make cheese. It's my hobby. They don't bother anyone, so why not?"

At the public hearing, dozens of people spoke in favor of Snowflake, Brownie, and goats in general. Enthusiastic supporters waved signs that proclaimed, "I'm pro-goat and I vote." One lone voice did rail against goats. She was a woman known around city hall for her rants against off-leash dog parks, and while she hated dogs in the city, she seemed to hate goats even more. She began with rather sensible concerns, such as goats jumping on fancy cars, but soon swayed off the road of rationality into descriptions of goats wandering into schools and pooping on desks, and goats heading into bars and drinking too much beer. There was also something about a pig named Wilbur who was some sort of barfly. This was a stroke of sheer luck—a coup that I could not have planned or even imagined. More persuasively than any highly paid Washington lobbyist, she convinced her audience that people opposed to goats in the city were certifiably nuts.

From this meeting on, the legalization of mini-goats was a slam-dunk. The committee voted unanimously in favor of goats, and the city council, upon hearing their recommendation, stamped the new ordinance with their approval. The ordinance stated that mini-goats were to be considered small animals, in the same category as cats and dogs. They would have to be 100 pounds or smaller, would require a license, would have to be disbudded and, if male, neutered.

I was incredibly lucky. Phyllis Schulman, my first contact at city hall, was an avid lover of animals and goat cheese. The health department's veterinary epidemiologist kept goats (she lived in the country), and Seattle is a tolerant, animal-loving city. But in other places, you may encounter some tough opposition. When you do, try to remember to stay calm. You simply want to keep goats. They are your hobby, and contrary to what people may say, they are not smelly or violent and are no more likely to spread disease than dogs or cats. In addition, remember that there are people out there who would keep goats irresponsibly. To address this issue, you can remind people that laws are in place to address problems such as noise, trespass, animal cruelty, and property damage. If someone has a loud goat that is bothering neighbors, those neighbors will be able to oust those noisy goats through the existing noise regulations.

Lastly, there is the issue of fairness. If dogs and cats are allowed, why shouldn't goats be? Dogs have very sharp teeth and are sometimes aggressive. They also sometimes bark loudly. Cats have no concept of property lines and cross them without remorse to attend to their business affairs in neighboring vegetable gardens and sandboxes. Yet despite these indiscretions, we allow dogs and cats. Shouldn't we allow goats too?

Ending Goat Intolerance in Your City

To find out if goats are legal where you live, the best place to start is with the zoning or planning department of your municipality. Most rules against goats come in the form of zoning regulations. Ask for a copy of the rules, so you know exactly what they say. Seattle's rules were quite specific about swine, which, except for a clause allowing potbellied pigs, were expressly not allowed. (Apparently, some lawmakers in the past had it in for pigs.) However, the rules did not mention goats specifically. Rather, they stated that farm animals, such as "cows, horses, and sheep," were prohibited on properties of less than 12,000 square feet. Often, there are setbacks involved in the farm animal rules. For example, the rule might say something like "farm animals must be kept 250 feet from any property line or any building."

DO GOATS HAVE RIGHTS IN YOUR CITY?

Here are some questions to ask your zoning department officials:

- Are there any rules on the books that specifically stipulate whether goats are allowed or not?
- Are there any rules on the books that regulate the keeping of farm animals?
- Do the rules define what a farm animal is?
- Do the rules regarding the keeping of goats or farm animals specify a minimum lot size? (For example, many areas will allow you to keep goats only if you have an acre or more of land. The amount of land required by different municipalities is highly variable.)
- Are there setbacks? (For example, some cities may allow goats but require that they be kept a certain distance from the property line or buildings.)
- Do the rules say anything about the size of animal that can be kept?
- If goats are not allowed, is there any way to get a formal exemption? If so, what is the process and cost for obtaining an exemption?

You may get lucky and find that goats are not prohibited in your city. Lots of places, like San Francisco, California, and Portland, Oregon, somehow never got around to passing laws preventing goats. If goats are not mentioned specifically in your city's zoning code, you may be able to work with members of the planning department to convince them that your goats are not farm animals. If you live in a city with forward-thinking elected officials or administrators, you might even convince them that their anti-farm-animal rule is culturally biased.

Sadly, chances are your city will have a rule specifically stating that goats are not allowed. If this is the case, your next step is to investigate how your neighbors feel about your getting goats, and to assess your existing relationship with your neighbors. If you are going to legalize goats, you are going to need neighbors who will stand up and say of you, "Yes, I know Jane. She's a fine neighbor and citizen of this city, and she should be able to keep goats. I live next door to her, and I wouldn't mind a goat in her yard one bit." If you don't have good relations with your neighbors, you likely will have a *very* hard time legalizing goats.

The Benefits and Drawbacks of the Secret Goat Garden

Although I do not support lawbreaking in general, I doubt I would ever have been able to legalize goats had I not broken the law. When I brought Snowflake and Brownie home and settled them into a hidden area of my backyard, with its shiny new goat shed and goat-proof fence, I had seen Seattle's city code and knew that farm animals such as "cows, horses, and sheep" were not allowed. While this was probably setting a poor example for my son, it did serve a purpose. My "goat garden room," unauthorized and in flagrant violation of the law as it was, allowed city council members, their assistants, and the media a chance to see, hear, and smell, firsthand, urban mini-goats.

Such a showcase is very important for silencing the ever-present "I grew up in the country with goats, and believe me, goats smell and don't belong in our town" know-it-alls. These people do not know how important it is to distinguish between unneutered male goats (bucks) and female goats (does) and neutered male goats (wethers). Unlike bucks, who are indeed *very* odiferous, does and wethers do not smell at all. In addition, unlike dog and cat poop, goat poop does not stink. Goat poop smells and looks quite similar to rabbit poop, and you seldom hear anyone complaining about rabbits smelling bad. A well-tended goat yard with well-tended goats is also helpful ammunition against those who argue that goats need acres to roam. Two contented goats will stomp out antigoat sentiment more effectively than any silver-tongued lobbyist.

The downside of setting up an illegal showcase is twofold. Breaking the law is a dicey exercise, ethically speaking, and if you fail in your attempt to legalize goats, you will have to find them a new home. This will be stressful for both you and the goats.

If you decide to get goats before they are legalized, it's a good idea to speak with your neighbors about it first. One of the things I did before beginning work on my goat yard was to check with my immediate neighbors to see if it would bother them if I kept goats in my backyard. I told them that if, after two weeks, the goats did bother them, I'd sell the goats. They agreed to this, and when six months later a woman who lived a quarter-mile away turned me in, both of my next-door neighbors stood up at city hall to testify on my behalf, saying that Brownie and Snowflake were model citizens and great to have around.

Lastly, and perhaps most importantly, if you create a goat garden room that is outside the law, do your very best to make it look good. Nobody likes an eyesore, and it's much easier to get people to accept pretty things than ugly ones. Beauty itself can be extremely and subtly persuasive. This is not to say that you have to make your goat yard beautiful. That would be tough. But do your best to keep it well tended and as scenic as possible.

Pets, Farm Animals, and Cultural Bias

When I first began to work on goat legalization with Phyllis Schulman, she suggested that I research the status of goats in other cultures to see if I could find a culture in which goats were considered pets. She explained that if we could demonstrate that the no-goat rule was culturally biased, we'd have an easier time getting the city council to vote in favor of allowing goats in the city. It was this assignment—this finding a culture in which goats were pets—that set me thinking about animals in a whole new way. What I found sheds light on why the topic of mini-goat legalization, which initially sounds so absurd, is really quite sensible and even *important*.

My research adventure went like this:

I started by speaking with a friend who had spent a few semesters in Greece during her college years. "Did the Greeks keep goats as pets?" I asked.

"Not exactly," she said "The family I stayed with kept a couple of goats, and the children played with them and even walked them around the neighborhood. They really loved those goats, and so I guess you could say that the goats were pets, except not really, because on Easter they ate them."

I then turned to someone from Africa, whom I knew from the YMCA. She said, "Well, in Africa, people have fun with the goats, and they do what they can to care for them, but when they get hungry, they eat them."

Hmm. In my search for goat cultural bias, I was discovering that people from other cultures were terribly uncivilized. So I decided to look to history. I found a book titled *Pets in America: A History*, by Katherine Grier. This had an interesting section about Native Americans and their dogs. "Depending on the tribe, Native American dogs were sources of muscle power pulling travois and sleds, representatives of cosmic forces that were sometimes sacrificed in religious ceremonies, fellow hunters, livestock herders, sources of protein, playmates for children and beloved companions." Here again, people were eating their pets.

It wasn't until I spoke with Fred Brown, who wrote his PhD dissertation on the history of farm animals in Seattle, that I started to see where I was tripping up in my thinking. He pointed out that the whole idea of a pet, and the whole idea of farm animals as distinct and different from pets, was culturally biased. To top this off, he pointed out that, historically speaking, the very concept of a pet, as distinct from farm animal or wild animal and deserving of a whole different set of ethics in terms of treatment, was a relatively new cultural bias.

Charlie Kubeniec holds Snowflake's newborn son, Seth Starkadder. *(Photo by Jennie P. Grant)*

In reading further, I discovered that the word "pet" did not even come into the English language until the early 1500s, and then it was used to describe "an indulged or spoiled child; any person indulged or treated as a favorite." According to Grier,

By the mid-sixteenth century, "pet" included animals "domesticated or tamed and kept for pleasure or companionship." The term was especially applied to orphan lambs that required raising by hand. It morphed into a verb, meaning to fondle an animal.... Noah Webster's American Dictionary of the English Language *of 1828 also defined "pet" as a "lamb brought up by hand," or "any little animal fondled and indulged"; as a verb it meant "to treat as a pet; to fondle; to indulge."*

Originally, the animals that we today consider pets were not considered pets at all. It used to be that all domestic animals were kept for reasons that had nothing to do with companionship. Cats caught rodents. Dogs herded, guarded, and pulled sleds and carts. Cows gave milk, and bulls gave beef. Hens laid eggs, and roosters gave roast chicken. Not only were all these animals not kept as pets, but they were kept in city and country alike. In the 1900s, farm animals were an integral part of city life. In his dissertation "Cows in the Commons, Dogs on the Lawn: A History of Animals in Seattle," Fred Brown describes early Seattle as a place where keeping cows and chickens was extremely common and of great importance to working-class women and children, who tended the flocks and helped graze the cows. He writes that in 1900, 750 of Seattle's 14,000 families kept cows, while dozens of others ran small in-town dairies. A majority of the families that kept one or two cows were led by single women. But as time went on and the city became denser, the home began to be seen not as a place of production, but as a place of consumption. Brown writes:

Increasingly, city-dwellers defined themselves by what they consumed rather than what they produced at home, as the growing importance of expansive green lawns showed. A key step in creating this new city was removing cows and horses.

And later:

As working animals left the city, the categories of livestock and pet became ever more divergent. A pet-livestock dualism replaced the pet-livestock borderlands. The divided regime took on increasing power. To remain in the city, animals had to become pets. The other choice was to become livestock and reside in the country.

The transformation of pet and livestock regulations took shape through the codes, covenants, and restrictions put in place by the movers and shakers behind housing developments. Along with specifying white-only middle-class neighborhoods, these restrictions explicitly banned all livestock, even chickens. What resulted was nonsensical. Farm animals, defined as animals who produced, were prohibited. Pets, defined as animals who did not produce, were allowed.

The Goat and I

The disappearance of farm animals in the city also had something to do with the development of the automobile. In the 1920s, the automobile changed from a toy for the rich into a viable and, ultimately, preferable, alternative to the horse. Before the car reigned supreme, horses were everywhere, just as cars are today. What's more, because they were everywhere, people were accustomed to managing their poop, living with their noise and odor, and providing them with housing, food, and exercise. Horses were so necessary that no one would have considered banning them. In addition, if you have horses filling your roadways and stables in your alley, you probably are not going to worry about a few cows and goats.

By the 1940s, when the car had replaced the horse, most jurisdictions had banned farm animals from urban areas, and the distinction between farm animal and pet was so clear in the minds of the lawmakers that the terms were used without definition in zoning codes across the nation. Pets were the animals that were allowed to remain in cities. Farm animals were the ones that got the boot. It was also at this time that farm animals began to represent the unsophisticated and passé. They were relegated to the country and came to represent all things rural. To the middle- and upper-middle-class Americans living within their white-only subdivisions, farm animals represented all that was coarse and ignorant. The idea of a sophisticated urban person keeping a goat was considered ludicrous, as was a rural person keeping a Pekinese. People found such mixing around so funny that it became the subject of some of the most lucrative comedies of the time.

From 1947 to 1957, a whole series of Ma and Pa Kettle movies were made. These were spin-offs using characters from Betty MacDonald's book *The Egg and I*. Though good-hearted, Ma and Pa Kettle were also portrayed as breeding like rabbits, opportunistic, and lazy. In the series of movies that followed the original, the Kettles move to a swanky suburb and bring their animals with them: a cow, chickens, goats, and a coonhound.

In 1962, a few years after the last Ma and Pa Kettle movie was made, *The Beverly Hillbillies* hit the air with the same comic premise—good-hearted rural people who hit it rich and move to a chic metropolitan area, bringing with them their backward ways.

In one episode, Jed Clampett is advised by his banker to invest in stock and, misunderstanding the banker's meaning, goes out and buys cattle, goats, and chickens and installs them in his tennis court.

By 1970, a generation after farm and urban life had become so distinct that few Americans thought much about their rural roots or had any real experience with rural life, the rural/city dichotomy as fodder for comedy was dropped. In 1971, CBS, as part of what was termed the "rural purge," canceled all shows with any remnant of rural life. *Green Acres, The Beverly Hillbillies, Hee Haw, Mayberry R.F.D.,* and even *Lassie* all got the ax. Television and movie executives of the age had no memories of the rural life and saw no reason to include it in their pop-culture fare. They were after a more sophisticated viewer, and nothing rural could possibly be sophisticated.

As small farms disappeared, factory farms replaced them. At first, this was seen as progress, but since the 1970s, the problems associated with factory farming have been coming to light. They degrade the environment through their use of herbicides and pesticides. They are inhumane in their treatment of animals, and they abuse the immigrant labor upon which they depend. As this information begins to spread, many people are longing for the reestablishment of the small family farms of the past. This is evident in the explosion in the number of farmers' markets in cities across the nation. The word "artisan" is now attached to many small-scale farm products, such as cheese. In addition, urban farming has taken hold as an engaging, healthful, and environmentally beneficial way to feed ourselves and strengthen our neighborhoods. What was once seen as ignorant and rural is now seen as progressive. What was once backward is now forward. And so steps forward the humble goat, into the modern city and across the farm animal/pet divide.

As the goat steps across, I hope she'll direct our focus to this divide and lead us to question it. People tend to treat animals in extremes—extremely well, as they would treat a human child, or extremely badly, as they would treat a commodity. For example, I was recently sitting in the bleachers watching one of my son's track meets when I was introduced to a woman named Betsy, who, I was told, also kept chickens. Betsy was effusive about her hens and went on at some length about how much she loved them. To illustrate her point, she told me that she had spent $800 to save the life of one of her hens. She was very proud of this fact. When the track meet drew to a close, she said goodbye and I heard her say to her children, "Okay, let's go. We'll stop at McDonald's on the way home and you can have McNuggets and a milkshake." This type of thinking cannot be good for anyone, except perhaps Betsy's hen. I am not advocating that we begin to eat our dogs, but having two codes of ethics for the treatment of animals is not good for animals and probably is not good for us either. Perhaps a pet/farm animal crossover—a pet dairy goat, for example—can help more Americans think about the issue and push for the more humane treatment of farm animals.

Noisy Goats

While I can rant about all the silly arguments used to oppose goats, there is one concern that is a serious one. That is the issue of noise. Some goats, just like some dogs, are noisy. Almost all goats will make noise for a few days when they first arrive at their new home. They'll miss their herd and will feel nervous. However, they should soon settle down. If they don't, you may need to find a new pair of goats.

I once had a problem with an Oberhasli goat. I brought her home a few months after the death of my goat Brownie. She was to be a companion for Snowflake. I'd always wanted a goat with beautiful ears, and I'd heard that Oberhaslis are the quietest of goats. I lucked out in finding an Oberhasli breeder just outside Seattle who had one of the nation's top herds and who also happened to have a young doe who had recently kidded and was in milk. The breeder was selling the doe because she was too small to be a show goat. This was perfect for me—a naturally mini-Oberhasli, from a champion herd, and in milk. I named her Maple.

Maple was an easy goat to love. She was beautiful, well behaved on the milking stand, tame, docile, and perfect in every way—at least in my eyes. Snowflake had ideas of her own. For whatever reason, Snowflake hated Maple. People have asked me, "But how do you know she hated her? What makes you think that?" Here's what. Snowflake constantly tried to butt Maple. If Maple wandered up to the manger where Snowflake was eating, Snowflake would butt her out of the way. If Maple was eating at the manger and Snowflake was on the other side of the goat yard, Snowflake would come over and butt her. If I came into the goat yard and Maple approached me for a pat, Snowflake would come over and butt her. As you might imagine, Maple developed a deep fear of Snowflake. For her part, Snowflake was just plain mad. How could such a weenie and a sissy of a goat dare to share her home? Perhaps because of Snowflake's ill treatment of her, and perhaps just because she had vocal tendencies, Maple cried out much of the day.

After the first few days, I told myself that with time this would all get smoothed over. However, the crying continued, and after a month I said to myself, "Perhaps this is just going to take more time than I thought." After several months, my neighbor said to me, in a gentle but stern manner, "Jennie, Maple is getting me upset. She sounds so unhappy. You need to do something about the situation."

I tried to get Maple to quiet down. I bought an anti-bark collar made for dogs that sprayed citronella juice when the microphone on the collar was activated by noise. I tried a collar that made an ultrasonic noise that dogs don't like. I even tried an electronic zap collar, putting it on the lowest setting. These efforts just made Maple more unhappy. I finally gave up, and when Snowflake gave birth to a daughter to serve as her companion, I sent Maple off to the country, where she is now living happily with a herd of other Oberhaslis. She has even won a red ribbon from a county fair.

It's interesting to note that Maple is an Oberhasli, a breed that is said to be the quietest. Nubians are said to be the loudest of all the breeds, and there is something about the tone of their bleat that is annoying to many people. So while going by a breed's reputation is a good place to start, breed alone will not guarantee a quiet goat.

Though I can't know for sure, I think Maple would have been quieter if she'd been with a goat who accepted her and offered some affection. According to her new owner, Maple is now quiet. For this reason, in looking for a goat, it's smart to buy a bonded pair, like two sisters or a mother and daughter.

It's also important to note that many female goats make noise when they go into heat. (Snowflake is an exception to this rule. Snowflake almost never makes noise.) Goats go into heat every eighteen to twenty-one days from September through February. Heats last anywhere from twelve to forty-eight hours. While most of your neighbors will have their windows closed this time of year, it is still wise to have a goat shed into which you can lock your noisy goats to help muffle their noise should they bother anyone. This issue of heats is also a good reason to keep wethers (neutered males) instead of females if you want goats as pets only and are not interested in milk.

A number of the city goat owners I have known have inadvertently taught their goats to be noisy. This is surprisingly easy to do. What happens is that when you first bring your goats home, they will cry because they do not like changes, especially changes involving moving away from their herd. New goat owners, in an effort to soothe their unhappy livestock, go out and offer pats and scratches under the chin. The goats then quiet down, the new owner walks away, and the whole sequence of events repeats itself. Soon the goats have learned that when they cry they get affection.

In an interesting cultural collision, my animal-loving friend Kate (she relocates rats instead of killing them) called an experienced country goat keeper, Jessie, to see how she handled the problem of noisy goats. Jessie said, "I just shoot 'em with my BB gun." While Kate couldn't bring herself to shoot her goats with BBs, she saw the logic in Jessie's approach and decided to try consequencing her goats with a hose. She also made sure to reward their quiet behavior by heading out and giving them attention only after they'd been quiet for a spell.

Interestingly, another friend, Melissa, tried the water consequence approach on her goat Molly, using a squirt bottle of the type that people use to discipline cats. She was surprised when, after being sprayed, Molly passed out cold. Some goats *really* hate to be squirted, and it's probably a good idea to consequence these goats in some other fashion.

Seattle's Goat Rules

There is a great deal that Seattle's goat legalization ordinance got right, but being the first of its kind in the nation, it could do with some revisions gained from thoughtful hindsight. Seattle's zoning code now defines mini-goats weighing 100 pounds or less as small animals, in the same category as dogs and cats. The preexisting law prohibits owning more than three small animals. Thus, according to Seattle law, you can keep two goats and a dog; or a dog, a cat, and a goat; or two cats and a dog; and so on, but you can't keep two dogs and two goats. Seattle's code also stipulates that goats cannot have horns, and that any male goat residing within the city be neutered. People are prohibited from walking their goats in public except for transportation purposes.

THE ISSUE OF SIZE

But what exactly is a mini-goat? Some people consider mini-goats to be Nigerian Dwarves and African Pygmies. Others consider them to be goats with at least 25 percent Nigerian Dwarf parentage. Still others consider them to be unusually small goats, like a runt of a standard dairy breed. In retrospect, it makes more sense to drop the word *mini* and simply have a weight limit for goats (which wouldn't apply to pregnant goats). Seattle's ordinance requires that goats be no larger than 100 pounds. This is perhaps too strict. I'd raise the size limit to 130 pounds. That would allow people to have many different types of standard dairy breeds—the goat would just need to be relatively small for its breed. Given that some dogs are 130 pounds and there is no size limit for dogs, it seems fair that people should be able to keep 130-pound goats.

THE NO-WALKING RULE AND THE STARTLING OBESITY EPIDEMIC AMONG INNER-CITY GOATS

About a year ago, my friend Anna confided in me that she was tired of people making comments about her goat, Gladys, like "Wow, that's sure a fat goat!" I told her that people just didn't understand that goats have big bellies, and that a large belly on a goat meant a nice big rumen, not excess fat. We'd have this conversation every few weeks. Then one day, while Anna was out of town and I was caring for her goats, I took a good look at Gladys and noticed that she was beyond round. The problem was not just that of a nicely developed rumen. I mentioned this, as delicately as possible to Anna, who hung her head and told me she was very worried that Gladys might have developed a serious weight issue. As time went on, Gladys got bigger and bigger, until one day she appeared so large that Anna decided to take action and bring her to the vet for some guidance.

And so it came to pass that one afternoon I got a call from Anna, who was quite distressed. Gladys had been diagnosed as "morbidly obese." Apparently, the vet (who is normally a kind man) sort of jumped back, stunned by the mere sight of Gladys's physique, as Gladys hopped from the back of Anna's station wagon. He then went on to say, "You shouldn't be able to balance a dinner plate on the back of your goat, and with your goat, I could hold a dinner party for four." The vet gave Anna a prescription: Gladys needed a half hour of cardio exercise every day. (He also gave Anna some tips on diet, which I cover later in Chapter 7.) In retrospect, this exercise prescription makes sense. Just as dogs, not to mention people, need a minimum of 30 minutes of exercise a day, so do goats. This story also points to the need for sensitivity training for large-animal vets.

The reason that Seattle's ordinance prohibits goat walking involves the unique nature of the way goats poop. Given the number of tiny pellets goats pop out over a half-hour period, it is difficult to pooper scoop after them. They do not land in a nice neat pile, but instead bounce, scatter, and roll all over the sidewalk. And while goat poop is not as smelly or messy as dog poop, it can, as can all poop, spread disease. To deal with this issue, while at the same time allowing goat owners to give their goats the exercise they need, it would have made more sense to require goats to wear berry bags while out in public. These are like the diapers horses wear in parades. It's interesting to note that Seattle's police horses do not wear diapers, and the police are not required to pooper scoop after them. Sadly, our world is full of goat injustice.

Note: Anna did as her vet directed. She changed Gladys's feed and began to walk her for a half hour every day. At first, Gladys balked and refused to budge. But with perseverance and patience, and considerable pushing and pulling, Gladys began to move. Within just a few months, she came to enjoy stepping out. Last I heard, Gladys was down 20 pounds and had just 25 more to go. She had also learned excellent leash manners that would put many dogs to shame.

Goats enjoy stepping out and it's good for their health.

Snowflake enjoys standing on the top of her goat yard stairs.

CHAPTER FOUR

SELECTING YOUR GOAT

AS IS OFTEN THE CASE WHEN YOU GO LOOKING for an animal, the first goat you see is the one you must have. And so it was that I came to feel that I had to have Brownie. In my Internet searches for mini-goats in Seattle, Brownie's herd, Glimmercroft, was the only relevant lead that popped up. And when I visited at her farm and saw her standing out in a field with the rest of her herd, I was hooked. Several months later I brought Brownie home, along with Snowflake, a doeling who belonged to a sister herd.

In retrospect, I was extremely lucky. Brownie belonged to Laura Workman, who had established her 1-acre Glimmercroft farm just thirty minutes north of Seattle. Laura had been trying to find or develop a smallish goat who could produce significant amounts of rich milk year round. She'd begun with Nigerian Dwarves and had had bad luck—hers had terrible lactation duration (they wouldn't give milk for more than a few months once their kids left), their small teats made milking slow and awkward, and they kicked and protested whenever she laid a hand on their teats to milk them. She ended up deciding on La Manchas because of their sweet, quiet nature and rich milk.

By crossing them with Nigerians, she was able to create a goat with richer milk, strong production, good teat size, good milking stand manners, and good lactation duration. When I met Laura in 2006, she had been studying goats and their breeding and care for ten years, and the results were impressive. She had developed the perfect type of goat for my needs—efficient milk producers who were quiet and whose milk was of premium quality.

While I lucked out in stumbling upon the perfect goats, I also lucked out in finding Laura. She was able to advise me about what to feed my goats, calmed me when I jumped to the conclusion that the mosquito bite on Brownie's teat was breast cancer, and talked me through rescuing my goats after they broke into the chicken coop and gorged themselves on chicken feed (which is so rich it gave them diarrhea). To this day, five years later, I still call Laura for advice, and she always takes the time to answer.

Goat Considerations

If I had not stumbled upon Laura's herd and instead had gone to visit someone with pet-quality Nigerians, I would probably have fallen in love with two very cute Nigerians, brought them home, bred them, failed to get much milk, and been forced to abandon my entire goat venture. Thus, this story is a roundabout way of explaining that breed matters. Decide on the type of goat you want *before* you go visiting any farms with goats for sale.

If you want a goat to provide your family with milk, don't pick one based on the cuteness of her ears. Find one who will produce an adequate amount of milk over a long period of time. Also keep in mind ease of milking. Milking a goat with the tips of your fingers and getting just teaspoonfuls with each squirt is going to get old very quickly. As you flip through websites on different breeds, remember that looking for a goat is similar to looking for a life partner. You must not let yourself be swept away by good looks. If you do, you could be in for some serious trouble. Look for qualities that will sustain your farmer/goat relationship for the long term. Namely, you want a quiet goat with a nice udder, big teats, and a long lactation duration who will also be a good and doting mother to her kids.

When selecting a goat, you'll want to keep in mind that even if you have read several books, which you should, you will still have questions. For this reason, don't just consider the goat—consider the person who owns that goat as well. This is the person who can demonstrate and help you trim hooves and who can advise you when you have questions. Also, make sure you are buying from someone who has goat milk from his or her own goats in the refrigerator. Otherwise, you may end up with two lovely pet goats who are very poor milkers. In addition, someone who isn't milking his or her goats probably won't be able to answer your milking-related questions.

You will need to take your doe to a stud buck every year, perhaps more than once if you read the signs of heat incorrectly or the breeding doesn't take. And you're not going to have much time to plan these trips. One morning, your goat will be crying more than usual, or flagging (a quick twitching of the tail), and you'll need to pop her into your car and drive all the way out to the stud buck's farm. For this reason, you shouldn't get a goat for whom there are no suitable mates within an hour or two drive.

Although books are a good source for learning about different goat breeds, so are county fairs. These usually take place in the late summer and fall and are a great place to see several types of breeds, meet breeders, and talk to experienced goat keepers firsthand.

Once your research is complete and you're ready to head out to goat farms to look at kids and does, don't go dewy eyed—stay alert, observe, and ask questions.

Find out about the milk and milking potential:

⚉ **Ask for a taste of the milk** from the mother of the doeling you are considering.

⚉ **Take a look at the mother's teats.** Would you need to milk her with your fingertips? The teats should be approximately the same size; are they?

⚉ **How do the people selling the goat do the milking—by hand or by machine?** Milking a goat with small teats is easy to do with a machine but very difficult to do by hand. Milking machines cost upward of $1,500 and involve significant amounts of cleanup, so unless you have several goats, you will most likely milk by hand, and teat size will matter.

⚉ **Also, sci-fi fantasy as it sounds, check the number of teats!** Some goats have more than two teats, a trait that can be passed down to future generations. You should not breed a three- or four-teated goat. Extra teats can get in the way of your milking. Extra teats that do not produce milk can confuse kids, who may persist in trying to nurse that teat and go hungry as a result.

⚉ **If the goat is in milk, ask to milk her.** Even if you aren't an accomplished milker yet, you can get a feel for how your hand fits to her teat and check to see if milk comes out of only one place on each teat. Some goats have extra orifices in their teats, and some teats have orifices that are extremely tight. You'll need some experience to know whether this is the case. If you have a friend who is an experienced milker and you are looking at a doe in milk, see if your friend will come with you to help evaluate the "milkability" of the goat who has caught your eye.

⚉ **Does the goat have horns?** Horns are not recommended for dairy goats. A horned goat could easily pierce the udder of her companion and thereby end a promising dairy career.

Find out about the general health and care of the herd:

- ❧ **Does the herd as a whole look well nourished?**

- ❧ **Listen.** Is the herd making much noise? What sort of noise is it?

- ❧ **Feel the goat you are considering buying.** Is she overweight, underweight, or just right? Goats often look very thin just after kidding, but be careful of goats who are extremely thin or extremely heavy.

- ❧ **Does the coat look healthy?** Bald patches and dullness suggest the goat may have some sort of nutritional deficiency or parasites.

- ❧ **Are the goat yard and shed relatively clean?** Are hay mangers and feed buckets arranged to keep out goat poop?

- ❧ **Ask directly whether the goat has had any medical problems** or whether anything is wrong with her.

- ❧ **Lastly, and perhaps most importantly, find out if the breeder is a potential mentor.** Ask the breeder if he or she will be able to answer questions should you have any after bringing the goat home. Ask yourself if the breeder is someone who you'd feel comfortable calling with questions.

The Best Milking Breeds for the City

This section gives the lowdown on the different breeds of goats that you may be considering. You will often hear about general tendencies of certain breeds, such as "Oberhaslis are quiet" or "The milk of Toggenburgs has a goaty flavor." Although such statements are often true, there will be exceptions.

The following are general descriptions of the most common milk goat breeds. I offer them as a very general guide. I describe the breeds from biggest to smallest.

NUBIAN

The Nubian attracts many a goat enthusiast with her gorgeous, pendulous, puppy-dog ears. Nubians have a Roman (convex) nose and a short, fine, and glossy coat. They have the richest milk of all the standard-sized dairy breeds and can be any color or pattern. The downside to Nubians is that they are loud and have a distinctive "cry." For this reason, Nubians aren't a good bet for the city.

Nubian *(Photo by Greenfire/Shutterstock.com)*

La Mancha

Alpine *(Photo courtesy House in the Woods Farm)*

LA MANCHA

La Manchas are popular for their calm temperament and rich milk. While you may not think that you want very rich milk, keep in mind that the higher the fat content of goat milk, the longer it will stay fresh and non-goaty tasting.

Upon meeting a La Mancha goat for the first time, most people ask, "What happened to her ears?" Nothing. La Manchas were bred to have very small ears. I read once that it was because parasites often hide in animals' ears and, by creating a small-eared goat, Oregon pioneers were able to lessen parasite problems. I think this may be one of those rural myths, because I have never heard of any ear-loving parasites. Some people have a problem with La Manchas because of their tiny ears. These people are shallow. Get to know a La Mancha and you will love a La Mancha.

ALPINE

A European breed, Alpines, also known as French Alpines, are extremely elegant and graceful. They have erect, upright ears, short or medium-length hair, and, according to the American Dairy Goat Association (ADGA) specifications, should have a straight face. The ADGA frowns on Alpines with Roman noses. Alpines produce a large amount

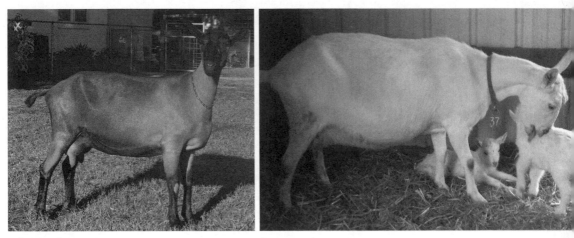

Oberhasli *(Photo by Rachel Anderson)*   **Saanen** *(Photo by Grace Lukens)*

of milk with relatively low milk fat. Dignified, relatively independent, and perhaps stubborn, these goats are task oriented (dairy-wise) yet still fun to get to know.

OBERHASLI

A Swiss breed, Oberhaslis have erect ears and are nearly always brown (a few are black), and have a black stripe running down their backs. Due to their coloring and ears, Oberhaslis look more like deer than any other type of dairy goat. They are known, like La Manchas, to have sweet and quiet dispositions. The face should be straight, and according to the ADGA, "a Roman nose is discriminated against."

As standard dairy breeds go, Oberhaslis are among the smallest. They are average milk producers in terms of volume. Their milk tends to be on the low side in terms of milk fat.

SAANEN

Another Swiss breed, the Saanen is always pure white. They are considered the Holsteins of the goat world, producing, on average, the largest quantity of milk. They have erect ears and a straight nose. They are the largest of the standard dairy breeds, so they probably aren't the best bet for the city. Even mini-Saanens are larger than 100 pounds.

TOGGENBURG

Yet another Swiss breed, Toggenburgs have upright ears and are light tan with white markings on their legs, ears, and faces. While they have the smallest ADGA size requirement, the average Toggenburg isn't particularly small. Toggenburgs have the

Toggenburg *(Photo by Liz Dawson)*   **Nigerian Dwarf**

lowest percentage of milk fat of all the dairy breeds, which may explain why their milk has a reputation for tasting goaty.

NIGERIAN DWARF

Nigerian Dwarf goats originated in West Africa. They are the smallest of the dairy breeds. Their ears are erect and alert, their hair is short and fine, and their face is dished or straight. Unlike other breeds of goats, which go into heat only during the months between September and February, Nigerian Dwarves can go into heat and breed successfully all year round.

The upside of Nigerian Dwarves is that their size is very manageable, making it relatively easy to take them out for a stroll around the neighborhood. (It is difficult to walk a 130-pound goat who wants to go in a different direction than you do.) Nigerians will also be easier to transport to the vet or the stud buck.

The downside of Nigerian Dwarves is that they produce less than half as much milk as a standard dairy goat, and they generally have very small teats. It is much harder to milk a small-teated goat than a large-teated goat. Much less milk comes out per squirt, and it can be difficult to keep your extra fingers out of the way of the milk stream and prevent it from squirting all over you. Milking a small-teated goat can easily take you twice as long as milking out the same quantity of milk from a larger-teated goat. Given that you will probably milk twice a day every day of the year, the problem of small teats is a serious one. If you are determined to get a Nigerian, meet her mother and examine her teat size. Also, make sure that whoever you buy her from has goat milk in the

African Pygmies *(Photo by Terri Nii)* **Kinders** *(Photo by Liz Lawley)*

refrigerator. Because of the popularity of Nigerian Dwarves as pets, some lines have lost their dairy abilities. Buy your goats from someone who milks theirs regularly. There are some fine Nigerian dairy goats out there; the trouble is in finding them.

OTHER BREEDS GOOD FOR BACKYARDS

There are other breeds, not recognized by the ADGA, that have gained popularity and should be part of your goat vocabulary.

African Pygmy goats are incredibly cute and little. However, they were developed as meat goats and don't have very good dairy qualities. Don't get an African Pygmy goat if you want to milk your goat. If you would like a pet, or a meat goat, or a companion for your dairy doe, an African Pygmy could be a fine choice.

Kinder goats are a cross between Nubians and African Pygmy goats. Those who have been developing the breed have done a good job of creating a smallish goat with good milk production, nice udder development, and good teat size. Being a cross between a goat with pendulous ears and a goat with upright ears, they often have "airplane ears," which are incredibly cute and look a lot like a nun's habit. However, be aware that kinder goats are usually, like their Nubian forebears, very loud. They are a fine choice for people in the country but a bad choice for people in the city, who have many neighbors within earshot.

Mini-goats are a cross between one of the original standard dairy breeds, such as Nubians or Alpines, and a Nigerian Dwarf. To be registered and qualify as a purebred mini-goat with the Miniature Dairy Goat Association, goats must be no more than 70

Mini-Nubian

Mutts

percent Nigerian Dwarf and no more than 70 percent the standard breed. Mini-goats were developed with the goal of creating smaller versions of the standard breeds, with richer milk and the Nigerian's ability to breed year round. They are generally between 95 and 120 pounds.

Part of the reason people began to look for smaller versions of the standard breeds was because over the last twenty years, judges at goat shows began favoring the larger contestants. The result of this preference for stature—bigger goats.

While for fear of my life I would not say this within earshot of a serious goat enthusiast, there are some good-quality **mixed-breed goats, or mutts,** out there. The only downside to these goats is that you often don't know their parentage, and their offspring can't fetch the same prices as purebred goats do. Purebred goats are somewhat different from purebred dogs in that the judging criteria are less a matter of pure fancy (with the exception of the nose and ear criteria). Dairy goats are judged in shows largely by their dairy qualities—udder size, udder attachment, and so on. So buying a goat who has done well in shows or is directly descended from such goats can help a novice evaluate a goat's quality.

On the flip side, sometimes show goats are overbred, and to my mind, there has to be some benefit in the genetic variation that comes with mixed breeding. If you want to buy a mixed-breed goat, just make sure you get to know well whoever is selling her. Are they milking the goat? Did they milk the mother? Is the person selling the goat serious about milk production and their herd? Will you be able to find a taker for your mutt goat's offspring?

BREED, SIZE, AND MILK PRODUCTION AT A GLANCE

A good-quality mini-version of any these goat breeds (that is, half Nigerian) can be expected to give approximately 75 percent of the standard milk amount listed. Note that milk production varies significantly among individual goats, so this 75 percent is just an estimate. The amount of milk a goat gives also varies according to the number of kids the goat birthed, her feed, and the number of times she has had kids. A goat will generally give more milk after her third set of kids than her second.

BREED	CUPS OF MILK PER DAY[1]	% MILK FAT	% PROTEIN	HEIGHT IN INCHES AT WITHERS[2]	WEIGHT IN POUNDS[3]
Nubian	9	4.6	3.7	At least 30	135
La Mancha	13	4.0	3.1	At least 28	130
Alpine	13	3.3	2.9	At least 30	130
Oberhasli	10	3.3	2.8	At least 28	120
Saanen	14	3.3	2.9	At least 30	135
Toggenburg	11	3.2	2.8	At least 26	120
Nigerian Dwarf	5	6.1	5.0	No more than 22.5	75

Source: American Dairy Goat Association
[1]These goats are milked twice a day, so for the amount of milk given per milking, halve the number shown.
[2]The withers is the ridge between the shoulders.
[3]This is the weight required of the breed to be shown competitively. Most show goats are much larger than this minimum weight, because judges like "stature."

The ADGA does have something called a recorded breed. This is a goat who has two pedigreed parents, but whose parents were not the same breed. These goats can be a good choice for someone who is concerned about purebred goats being inbred.

Other Factors in Choosing Your Goats

When choosing a pair of goats, you'll need to think about more than what breed would work best for you. Here are some additional points that are important to consider.

ALWAYS GET AT LEAST TWO GOATS

Goats are herd animals, and as such, each needs at least one full-time companion. Keeping a single goat is going to be stressful on the goat. What's more, a stressed and unhappy goat can cause trouble that only a goat could dream up. Lonely, stressed goats are more prone to diseases. Dogs, while they can get along with goats, don't make good goat companions, especially if they are spending much of their days and nights in the house instead of the goat yard. Sheep and horses can keep goats company, but goats like other goats best of all.

TRY TO GET TWO GOATS WHO ARE ALREADY BONDED

From the school of hard knocks, I learned that not all goats get along. As I mentioned earlier, when one of my first goats, Brownie, passed away unexpectedly, I brought home an Oberhasli named Maple to keep Snowflake company. I loved Maple. She was perfectly behaved on the milking stand and very affectionate. Snowflake did not love Maple and greeted her by smashing her against a fence. Although Snowflake and Maple arrived at a sort of détente, neither goat was happy. Maple always had to tiptoe around the yard in fear of Snowflake, and Snowflake had to expend a lot of energy stalking and ramming Maple. The stress upon both goats began to take its toll, and their health waned. After Snowflake had a daughter and Maple suffered the loss of triplets, I decided to find Maple a new home. She's flourishing now, and so is Snowflake, who is very happy to have the companionship of her daughter, Eloise. The two curl up and snooze together at the top of their stairs. Snowflake, who had been looking unwell during Maple's tenure, has blossomed ever since Maple's departure. Her coat has become shiny and lustrous and people have begun to comment on her good looks.

This is how I learned that not all goats get along. Goats will almost always get along well if they are siblings born at the same time or if they are mother and daughter. Thus, if you can find sisters or a mother-daughter pair, you'll almost be guaranteed peace in the goat yard.

Two young kids who are unrelated can usually learn to get along, but it can be difficult to find a suitable companion for a grown doe. In a larger herd, it's easier for goats who don't like one another to simply ignore each other. Finding a single companion for a single adult doe is often especially challenging. The best solution is to get the lone doe pregnant and hope for a daughter. In the meantime, a tiny African Pygmy wether (neutered male) can be good company.

KIDS OR ADULTS?

It is often possible to find a young doe who has already had kids, is in milk, and is trained on the milking stand. This is due to the preponderance of goat owners who suffer from a condition characterized by the following symptoms: They decide to keep the really fabulous doeling born to their favorite doe. Then, lo and behold, their second-favorite doe gives birth to an even more fabulous doeling, so they keep her too.

This pattern continues for several years, and then one day they look out their window, gaze out onto their goat yard, and are shocked to find—too many goats.

The prevalence of this condition is good for the new enthusiasts who, due to the laws of supply and demand, can pick up these fabulous does for the same price as an eight-week-old doeling who won't be giving milk for a year and a half. Buying an older doe is a good idea in that you know from the outset the quality of her udder and teats and her behavior on the milking stand. It may even be possible to buy a young doe and her new daughter together. This will enable you to have milk right away plus a cute little doeling who you can watch grow, and it will also ensure that you have a bonded pair. On the downside, if the doeling is not yet weaned, you'll have to tackle weaning her, which isn't difficult but calls for some persistence. Another downside of buying a doe in milk is that you will be diving into goat ownership all at once rather than easing into it.

YOU MAY WANT JUST ONE DAIRY GOAT AND A LITTLE WETHER COMPANION

If you don't have a large family and can't use two goats' worth of milk, you may want to get one standard-sized dairy goat and a small companion wether. Wethers don't go into heat, so you won't have the problem of them being noisy around breeding season. Also, they are smaller, so they'll be easier to handle and won't need to eat as much. Because wethers can be bossy, it is important, if you have a dairy goat, that the wether be significantly smaller than your doe. Otherwise, your wether will spend much of his time hogging the food and pushing your productive goat away from the nourishment that is so critical to her milk production and/or her developing kids. With one wether and one standard dairy goat, you can get the milk you want, do so without having to squeeze it out of tiny teats, and have a cute little goat to boot.

THE CITY IS NO PLACE FOR A STUD BUCK

Many people who plan to breed their goats assume that they need a stud buck. These people are *wrong*. You do not want a stud buck in the city or the suburbs. Stud bucks get *very* smelly during rutting season (October through February), and they are incredibly virile and sort of rascally. Stud bucks are usually kept in fields with other stud bucks and spend their days preening (by urinating on themselves) and butting one another in the hopes of winning the heart of some passing doe. Because they are so smelly and so rowdy, even their doting owners steer clear of them. If you pat a stud buck in rut on the head, you will not be able to get the smell off your hand for several days. As a result, many stud bucks get a bit lonely for human companionship during rutting season. When not in rut, they actually can look sort of nice and behave normally. But more than half the year *is* rutting season, and during that period they simply don't have the personal hygiene habits required for city life. In short, you should not get a male-female couple as your two goats. While it may seem sort of sad, your doe is going to need to settle for a one-afternoon stand. Long-term relationships of the connubial kind are not in the cards for city goats.

Keeping a stud buck also doesn't make economic sense. Feeding a stud buck for a year costs several hundred dollars, whereas it costs only between $50 and $75 to bring your doe to a stud buck and have him work his magic.

BOTTLE-FED VS. DAM-RAISED GOATS

You will often hear it said that bottle-raised kids are much tamer and friendlier than dam-raised kids (goats raised by their mothers). Bottle-raised kids are taken from their mother at birth and given a bottle by humans. When they are about a week old, they are returned to their herd, where they get along with their mother but never nurse from her teats and never really know her as a mother. People raise goats like this to better control the amount of milk the kids get, prevent the transfer of a disease called CAE, prevent the kids from accidentally biting their mother's teats, and increase the kids' comfort with humans. Every once in a while, a mother goat will reject her kids and bottle-feeding becomes necessary.

The trouble with bottle-feeding is that it breaks the bond between mother and baby, which is really a very beautiful bond to see. It's also more work, and kids on the bottle can experience more health problems on the whole than kids raised by their mothers.

Bottle-raised kids tend to be tamer than dam-raised kids and will probably bond to you more readily. However, this isn't always a good thing. A goat who is too strongly bonded to humans may cry out for you as she would for her mother. You want a goat that is relaxed around you and happy to see you but even happier to be sitting with her companion goat. Dam-raised goats who have been handled gently and regularly are plenty friendly and may have a slight tendency to be quieter. With all this said, my goat Snowflake was bottle raised and is the quietest goat I know.

Lastly, people can dam-raise kids *and* spend lots of time with them, holding them, giving them treats, and so on. When this happens, the kids turn out to be as tame as my pug dog, Eddie.

Large with kids, Snowflake is untroubled by the busses, bikes, and cars going about their city business on the street below.

CHAPTER FIVE

YOUR GOAT YARD

"THE PRUDENT MAN DOES NOT MAKE the goat his gardener," says an old Hungarian proverb, and it certainly is hard to imagine how a goat could beautify your garden. However, a farm animal "garden room" adds tremendous interest to your yard, and with a handsome goat shed and lots of wood chips or straw on the ground, it can lend a certain charm. Goats are always up to something interesting—relaxing in the sun, chewing their cud, or trying to figure out a way to break out of their yard and eat your prize rosebushes.

Goat Space Requirements

My goat yard is about 400 square feet, and within that I keep two goats. Anything smaller than that doesn't give the goats enough room to move around. Even if you have Nigerian Dwarves or African Pygmies, they will still need at least 400 square feet. If you have more space to give your goats, they will appreciate it greatly. You may see other numbers thrown around in books, but none of them were developed in a scientific manner. All are simply numbers thought to be about right by the people writing books about goats. Ditto for my recommendation.

This minimum square footage also assumes that you will not have two sets of goat kids in your goat yard at once. You will need to keep your goat kids for eight weeks, so if you have only 400 square feet and your goats give birth within two weeks of one another, each having two kids, you will suddenly have six goats within your 400 square feet. If each of your goats has three kids, you will have eight goats within your 400 square feet. That is *too* many goats. Therefore, if you have only 400 square feet for your goat yard, space the kidding of your goats such that your first set of kids will have left the nest before the second set is born.

SITING

Many people, given the layout of their yard, won't have much choice as to where to site their goat yard. But if you do have options, you'll want to keep some of the following issues in mind.

- **Convenience and access.** Much of goat keeping involves hauling. You will be hauling in loads and loads of wood chips and giant bales of hay and alfalfa pellets. You will be hauling out yards and yards of compost. If you can site your goat yard so that you can bring in loads by truck rather than by wheelbarrow or bucket, you will save yourself days' worth of backbreaking labor.

- **Water source.** You'll need to change your goats' water every day. If you can, site your goat yard near a water spigot, or make sure you can easily reach it with a hose.

- **Drainage.** Goats can tolerate a bit of mud here and there, but if they are regularly sinking an inch or two into mud, they may develop a bacterial disease called hoof rot. Even if you have good drainage, you will still need to cover your goat yard with a few inches of wood chips or straw to help protect their hooves from mud. With poor drainage, even wood chips may not suffice.

- **Shade and heat.** While goats can tolerate a freezing night with little trouble, they are less tolerant of heat. Make sure that your goat yard is situated such that there is always a patch of shade available.

- **Plants and shrubs.** Many ornamental plants, especially rhododendrons and laurel, are highly toxic. Make sure that none of these plants are within nibbling or leaf-dropping reach of your goat yard.

- **Trees.** If you have a tree in the area where you plan to put your goat yard, your goats will eat it. They will begin by eating every leaf they can reach. Next, they will carefully, bite by bite, remove every stitch of that tree's bark. Your tree will not be able to survive this assault and will die. However, there are ways around this problem. If you wrap the tree's trunk with hardware cloth, the goats will not be able to eat the bark. They will get any overhanging branches, but if the tree is large, it should be able to survive this. If you can make it work, a tree in the goat yard adds beauty and provides shade.

Shape of yard. Your goat yard need not be square, oval, or rectangle. You can run two fences several feet apart around the perimeter of your yard, creating a sort of track. This will allow your goats to run laps. You will still need a larger paddock to house the goat shed and to allow them to mill around, but they will enjoy a few long runways to let fly.

View, part I. Consider giving the best view in your yard to your goats. Remember that you may well end up spending more time in your goat yard than in any other section of your garden, because you'll be there for milking, feeding, watering, and sweeping. While you're there, you'll enjoy the view too. Besides, goats will probably appreciate the view more than you do. They have rectangular eyes that enable them to keep an eye on the horizon. These sorts of eyes have got to give a good view a beauty boost.

View, part II. Remember that your goats can be the view. My friend Anna has a perfect view of her goat yard from her kitchen and dining room. This adds great interest to what she sees out her windows. She can watch the happenings of the goat yard while washing the dishes. What's more, her goats often liven up the conversation at the dinner table. Someone is always piping up with, "Hey, what is that goat up to?"

View, part III. Do you want passersby to be able to see your goats and/or reach in to touch and feed them? In some ways, it's nice to have the public come by and admire your goats. There were a small horse and a goat living near me, and parents with small children loved to visit them while out for a walk. The owners put up a sign asking people not to feed the goat, and people never did. But of course, there are people out there who will ignore any signs you post. A friend of mine who kept goats once discovered that someone had tossed into her goat yard a plastic bag containing rotten lettuce. Because plastic can get caught in the digestive system of a goat and block off important passages, it can be deadly. So while keeping a goat in plain view can be fun, it's also risky.

Chickens. Goats and chickens can cohabitate. If you already have chickens, or plan on getting some, you can allow them to share the same yard, provided you don't have more than about four chickens per 400 square feet. Goat kids have fun practicing their butting skills on chickens, and the chickens don't seem to mind it too much. If you do keep goats and chickens together, you'll need to make sure that your goats can't access the chickens' feed, since if a goat overindulges in chicken feed, she can contract enterotoxaemia and die (for more on chicken-goat cohabitation, see Chapter 13).

FENCING

There is an old Greek saying that goes, "It is easier to build a fence that can keep out water than a fence that can keep in goats." This is, of course, an exaggeration, especially since the invention of the stock panel, a truly wonderful fencing material intended for, as its name implies, livestock.

A goat fence should be at least 52 inches high. There are many suitable types of fencing materials, including cedar panel, chain link, and woven wire. However, unless you need the privacy offered by a solid cedar fence, stock panels offer the most advantages. They are more expensive than woven wire fences but are far easier to install and don't sag after years of goats rubbing up against them. Chain-link fencing can work well, but it too is extremely difficult to install, and if you decide to reposition your fence lines, it won't be easy. The approximate cost of each type of fence, not including the posts or gate, by the linear foot is $1 for welded wire, $3 for chain link, $3 for stock panel, and $7.50 for cedar panel.

Tom Clauson offers his goat Molly a treat through a wood and high-five stock panel fence.

Stock panels come in 16-foot lengths. They are constructed from heavyweight galvanized wire rods. The wire rods are welded at every intersection and are heavily galvanized with a thick zinc coating. There are three types of stock panels worth considering for goat fencing. The prices listed are those charged by my local feed store.

- **Cattle panels.** These are 52 inches high with divisions that are 6 by 8 inches: $36.

- **Combo panels.** These are 52 inches high with 6-by-8-inch divisions. The divisions are smaller along the bottoms of these panels, but not small enough to keep in chickens or young kids: $40.

- **High-five panels.** These are 5 feet high, and the divisions are 4 by 4 inches: $60.

The high-five panels are ideal in that they are 8 inches taller than the combo panels and have divisions that even day-old kids cannot crawl through. However, they are one and a half times the cost of the combo panels. Although the combo panels are great in concept, with the smaller divisions lower down, they don't actually work to keep kids from escaping. For cost and convenience, your best bet is to buy the cattle panels and attach welded wire fencing or chicken wire along the lower 2 feet of the panels when kids are young. You can also attach welded wire or chicken wire to the bottom of combo panels, but the cattle panels are less expensive.

Stock panel fences can be constructed in an afternoon, using steel farm posts and zip ties. The stock panel should be on the goat side of the post, so that when the goat pushes against the fence, the panel is supported by the post. The advantage of a fence made of farm posts and stock panels is that it can easily be moved with a fence-post puller and fence-post hammer. The downside is that it is not particularly attractive.

Stock panel can be incorporated into more traditional-looking fences using wooden posts and, if you want to get really fancy, boards along the top and bottom.

A WOOD CHIP FLOOR

One problem with keeping goats in a small space is that they readily destroy all vegetation, poop a lot, and in the end turn their home into a huge, muddy mess. For this reason, you need to lay down wood chips or straw on the goat yard's ground every four to six months. To cover a 400-square-foot area with wood chips 3 inches deep, you will need almost 4 cubic yards.

Arborist chips work especially well for goat yards because while they keep mud at bay, they will eventually break down. This is important, because after several years of laying down wood chips every four to six months, you will one day find yourself puttering around your goat yard and be surprised to notice that your fence posts have grown shorter. When this happens, you will need to rake off the top layer of arborist chips and dig out several inches of fabulously rich compost. If you aren't able to use all of the compost in your own garden, you should have no problem finding it a happy home—unless it is full of wood chips. This is why it's important that the chips you use eventually break down. Clearing out the compost is not something that needs to happen very frequently. I managed to go five years before I needed to take my goat yard back to its original height. However, when it is time to clear out the compost, you want it relatively free of wood chips.

Arborist chips are created when arborists take down trees and put them through a grinder, leaves and all. They are a better choice than cedar play chips, because the cedar chips break down too slowly. Arborist chips are also much less expensive than wood chips. Some arborists will deliver a load of wood chips for free. Others will charge to make a drop.

You need to be a little careful with arborist chips because they sometimes contain leaves of plants that are poisonous to goats. Thus, when ordering your chips you'll need to make sure they don't contain a large percentage of poisonous plants. In the Northwest, where laurel is ever present, you'll want to ask the arborist how much laurel is in the load. Generally, goats don't eat from off the ground, but if it's winter and there is little browse available, they'll eat those nice green laurel leaves and may get seriously ill.

SUMMARY OF GROUND COVER HAULING CHORES

If you have a 400-square-foot goat yard, you will need about 4 cubic yards of chips to create a 3-inch-deep layer.

You'll need to lay down chips every four to six months, depending on your climate, the number of goats you keep, and the size of your goat yard. When the ground is muddy, or you find yourself slipping, try stirring the layer of wood chips up with a pitchfork. If that doesn't help with the mud problem, it's time to lay down more chips.

Haul out the accumulated chip and goat poop compost before the level of your goat yard has risen to the point that your goats can jump the fence. For me, this took five years.

NOTE: Instead of 4 yards of wood chips, some people add a few bales of straw.

I have never used straw in my goat yard, but a friend of mine swears by it. If you do try straw, it may work better if you also have some chickens who will spend their days pecking and scratching at it, thereby helping to break it apart. This will prevent it from matting together and forming a nasty glob rather than friable compost.

If the space you have available for your goats is cement or asphalt, you will not need wood chips, but you will need to sweep up the goat poop every day and hose off the surface from time to time. Such a surface is in some ways very good for goats, as it can help wear down their hooves and make hoof trimming easier.

While I often wish my goats had an acre to roam, there is an upside to a very small goat yard. Without grass underfoot, your goats will not be able to eat any grass upon which they have pooped. This is how many of the internal parasites common to goats are passed and helps explain why urban goats tend to have fewer problems with parasites than their country cousins.

Don't worry about giving up one of the nicest sites in your yard to goats. You'll be spending lots of time there, so you'll be able to enjoy it too. *(Photo by Lori Eanes)*

Goat Yard Essentials

Once you've planned and sited your yard, and figured out fencing and flooring, it's time to lay out the essential elements of your goat garden room.

WATER

You'll want to change your goats' water every morning and when the days get warm, twice a day, so have a spigot handy near your goat area. If you don't, you can run a hose, but a spigot is best. You can hang your goat's water bucket on the stock panel divisions with a carabiner or from a hook screwed into a fence post. The bucket should be too high for your goats to poop into it yet low enough for them to reach and drink from.

If you keep chickens in your goat area, they can cause problems with the water bucket. They will, for reasons known only to them, eschew their own water supply placed conveniently at hen level and hop onto the rim of your goats' water pail. Because

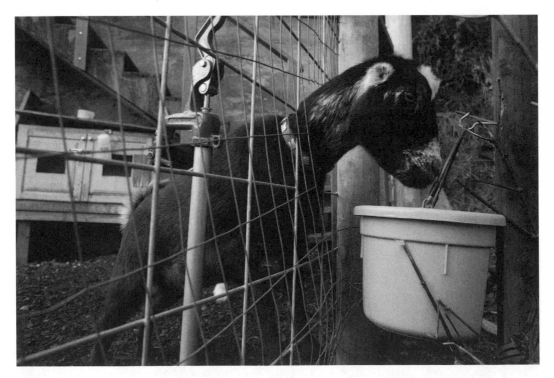

Hang water and alfalfa pellet buckets just outside the fence so your goats can reach their heads through to drink, but can't lean their muddy hooves on the rim and get dirt into their feed.

they usually have dirty feet, they'll inadvertently drop dirt into your goats' water. To solve this problem, you can hang your goats' water bucket on a hook attached to a post on the outer side of your goat fence. This keeps the chickens from perching on the bucket but allows the goats to reach their heads through the holes of the stock panel to get a drink. This simple system probably goes a long way in helping to prevent parasites.

ALFALFA PELLET BUCKET

If you keep dairy goats, at some point in their lives, you will likely need to offer them alfalfa pellets (see Chapter 7). The trouble with alfalfa pellets is that if you put them in a bucket, the goats will somehow manage to get poop in the bucket and then, wisely, won't eat the pellets. The best way to keep your alfalfa pellets safe from goat poop but still accessible for eating is to hang the bucket just outside the goat yard, as suggested in the previous section for the water bucket. If you use this system, you'll need to create a small slanted roof over the bucket to keep the alfalfa pellets dry.

FOLIAGE FEEDER

Because goats are mainly browsers, their preferred eating method is to reach up and yank leaves from trees. To give them a treelike structure from which they can tug their food, you can make a foliage feeder. You'll need two 8-foot fence posts and two

The foliage feeder replicates a bush and eating bushes is goats what live to do. Foliage feeders also prevent goats from spilling feed on the ground.

Top: A foliage feeder allows a goat to eat from either side. *Bottom:* Bungie cords and a fence can hold browse at goat level, but allow access from only one side.

pieces of stock panel, each about 3 by 4 feet in size. Set the posts several feet apart. Hinge the stock panel pieces together at the bottom with wire or zip ties, and then attach one of the panels to the posts. Set this stationary panel about a foot and a half above the ground. The second panel (not attached to the post) should be left to swing open and closed. You can clip it closed with a bungee cord. To load bramble or tree branches into the feeder, just remove the bungee cord, lay the edibles in the feeder, and then clip the panels back together with the bungee cord. The foliage feeder minimizes the number of leaves that fall on the ground, never to be nibbled at again; is easy to load and unload; and will give your goats the feeling of eating from a bush—one of their favorite pastimes.

HAY STORAGE BOX

Bales of hay are *big,* and they need to be kept dry. They can't be stored on a cement floor, or they will absorb moisture from the cement and go bad. In addition, your goats are going to go through a lot of hay, so it's nice to have a hay storage box near their manger. A manger is a device for dispensing hay. It holds the hay off the ground so that

Eloise travels down the ramp of her hay storage box. When it's sunny, she likes to nap on top of the box.

the goats can access it. A hay storage box in your goat yard makes it easy to replenish your goats' hay and can make a great piece of exercise equipment or serve as a raised sleeping platform for your goats. If you have room for hay storage in your goat shed, you may not need a hay box. However, it's nice to be able to buy several bales of hay at a time, especially if you pay for delivery. So unless you have a very large goat shed, a hay box or two will come in handy.

You can build a hay storage box out of 2-by-4s and plywood, or you can purchase a deck storage box. The inside dimensions of the box should be at least 52 by 24 by 24 inches. To create such a box from a single 8-by-8-foot sheet of plywood, you'll need to build the framing on the outside of the box. If the framing is inside the box, you'll need larger inside dimensions because interior framing will take up valuable space. Set the hay box a foot off the ground to prevent it from absorbing moisture from below. To do this, you'll need to create a sort of table with pressure-treated 4-by-4s as legs. Set these legs about a foot into the ground for stability.

Rubbermaid makes a perfectly sized deck storage box (54.5 by 26.5 by 25 inches) with seat for about $150. It's available at many big-box hardware stores and in some ways works better than a plywood box, because it's difficult to make a plywood box that doesn't leak, and keeping your hay dry is extremely important.

MILKING PAGODA

A milking pagoda (see photo on page 126) is just a fancy way to describe a structure that provides a roof over your milking stand. It's best to have your milking stand in an area within the goat yard, or just outside it, that is sheltered from the rain, for the comfort of both you and your goat. I used to milk in my goat shed, but the space was small and cramped, and there was goat poop all around. Having read that celebrity sustainable farmer Joel Salatin butchers outside, and that this method was found to be more sterile than a stainless steel–lined butchering room, I began to think about how a person could build a covered outdoor milking area. When I dismantled my old chicken coop and was left with a 5-by-8 foot roof, I decided to set it atop four tall posts to make a sort of milking pagoda. This worked beautifully. The posts I used were pressure treated and 10 feet long. Using a fence posthole digger, I set them 2 feet into the ground. I set the milking stand on the ground, wedging a board under a leg or two for stability.

A milking stand is a table with a stanchion attached to one end to hold the goat in place. Chapter 11 discusses other types of milking stands.

GOAT PLAY STRUCTURES

Climbing is one way that goats have fun! All goats appreciate things to jump up on and down from, and they like things that are up high on which to nap. When not napping on the platform, a goat will enjoy standing on it and keeping other goats from joining her through frequent butting. When I first added a plywood hay box to my goat yard, I worried it would get in the goats' way, but they quickly made use of it. They would jump on and off it, and when they got tired of that, they'd lie on top of it to take a nap. I've since added a ramp with hinges that the goats enjoy for climbing up onto their box. I've seen other people use old sets of wooden stairs. Goats love climbing stairs, especially if those stairs end in a platform large enough to stand or sleep on. Many goats also enjoy giant wooden spools. These you can often find at scrap metal recyclers. Telephone, cable, and electric companies also often give them away. If you already have a large rock or boulder in your goat yard, you could incorporate that into the goats' climbing structures.

You do not want so many play structures that your goat yard becomes an obstacle course, but you should have at least one play structure per adult goat. For a pair of goats, this means you'll need a set of stairs and a raised platform or two raised platforms. Anything more would be appreciated by your goats but is not required. Make sure when adding a play structure not to place it too near the fence. You don't want your goat to climb it and then be able to hop out of the goat yard.

Rosie stands at the threshold of her luxury goat shed. To her right is a doorway tall enough for humans to enter.

CHAPTER SIX

THE GOAT SHED

YOUR GOATS WILL SPEND MOST OF THEIR TIME outside in their yard, but they will need a shelter from rain, snow, and strong winds.

Goats can tolerate very cold temperatures, but not if they are wet, and not without some protection from wind. Your goats will need a dry floor, four walls, and a roof. A goat shed will also come in handy if your goat is in heat and making a lot of noise. To spare your neighbors her wailings, you can close her in the shed until her instinct to yell for a mate has waned. Goat sheds are also important at kidding time. People with a lot of land often have a separate kidding stall, but you can make do without one if you have only two or three goats and a goat shed.

Shed Structure and Size

Your goat shed can be a very simple structure—four walls, a roof, and a doorway. A window and electricity are nice but not necessary. You'll sometimes need light in the shed, but you can make do with a head lamp if you don't have electricity. It is very important to build your goat shed tall enough to allow you to stand. There is no chore worse than shoveling deep bedding out of a goat shed when you are hunched over and frequently banging your head.

Two to three goats will require a goat shed that is at least 6 feet by 8 feet. This will give each of your goats room to lie down or mill about without feeling crowded during long, stormy nights. It also gives you some space to place a small hay manger and milking stand if you choose to milk in your goat shed (although I recommend an open-air milking pagoda, as described earlier). It's best to have a gate to your goat shed so that

The new, official Goat Justice League state-of-the-art goat shed

Back view

Front view

Birds'-eye view

Bird's-Eye View Key

a. Storage for one hay bale
b. Storage for containers of goat chow, chicken feed, and alfalfa pellets
c. Chicken roosting area with cleanout hatch in floor. Water bottle hangs on door.
d. Goat milk stand and stool
e. Hay feeder mounted on wall
f. Removable partition made from metal stock panel, with inset access door. Use partition to separate kids from mother.
g. Fold-down bench, with storage for optional second hay bale beneath (flip up when stock panel divider is in place).
h. Chicken nest box

you can lock one goat in while you are milking the other. If you don't, the loose goat will try to get into the treat you are feeding the goat being milked. A gate is also useful at kidding time when you don't want the goat who is giving birth to be bothered by her companion. It's even better if you can equip your goat shed with a door. This way, if you find yourself with a goat who is noisy when in heat, you can muffle the noise by locking up the culprit until she quiets down.

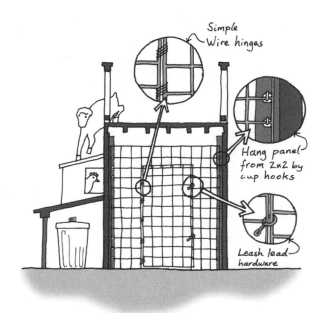

Wooden floors work well in goat sheds. If you leave $1/8$-inch gaps between the floorboards, excess moisture (goat pee) can drain through the gaps. You

Cross section with kids area divider: The divider is only in place when the kids need to be separated from their mother at night (from four days to eight weeks old).

can use plywood for flooring, but if you do, drill $1/4$-inch holes in a grid pattern every 6 inches. I know of a goat shed in which the builders laid down vinyl flooring to protect the floor underneath. This left *no* drainage. To offset the problem, the owners use additional wood shavings. Many goat owners swear by cement floors and simply sweep out the goat poop and pee every morning and hose it down from time to time. This method works if you don't mind sweeping out the goat shed once a day. It also requires you to have sleeping platforms inside the shed, since cement floors can be cold and you don't want your goats to have to lie in puddles of pee.

The wooden prefab garden sheds you see for sale at hardware stores can work well for goats. They are nice in that should you ever sell your goats, you can easily deconstruct them and sell them to someone else. Sadly, these sheds are very expensive and not especially attractive.

If you are handy or have the money to hire a carpenter to build a fancy goat shed, consider building the new Official Goat Justice League state-of-the-art goat shed. This innovative new design revolutionizes the goat shed of old. While keeping the goats warm and dry, it also doubles as a play structure, increases the goats' living area with a

This manger enables goats to nibble from either side.

rooftop deck, and includes a chicken coop, a hay storage box, and a small shed to store chicken and goat feed. It also provides a covered outdoor milking and feeding area for better sanitation. Inside, it has stock panel gates on hinges that fold out from the walls to create a separate kidding stall or a place for the kids to spend the night.

The Manger

Your goats are going to need hay available to them at all times, so you'll want a manger. As noted previously, a manger is a device for dispensing hay. Because of the way goats eat, mangers that work for goats are nothing like the horse manger that Baby Jesus is said to have napped in during his infancy. Baby Jesus would be very upset to have lain in a goat hay manger. In fact, he would have been so upset and traumatized by the experience that he may not have grown into the big-hearted person he is purported to have been.

The ideal goat manger requires some work on the part of the goat to pull out the hay. If you use the type of manger built for horses, your goats will quickly take all of the hay out of it, dump it on the ground, and then poop, pee, and stomp on it. This effectively takes horse hay mangers out of the picture.

You can build a highly effective and simple manger with high-five stock panel (the type with divisions spaced in a 4-inch grid), a 2-by-4, and two 6-foot-long 4-by-4 posts. Such a manger also keeps chickens from hopping in to nap, lay eggs, and possibly poop. To build this type of manger, assemble a square frame using the 2-by-4. It should be 2 feet long, 2 feet wide, and 4 inches deep. Next attach a piece of stock panel to the bottom. Then attach a second piece of stock panel to the top of your box, but attach it only at one end, using a U-shaped round wire nail so that the panel can swivel open and closed. Mount the manger between two poles, put in a flake of hay, and close it, using a bungee cord. This manger allows goats to eat hay from either side.

You can also buy plastic or metal mangers from most feed stores, through goat supply catalogs, or from online farm supply companies. See the Goaty Resources section at the end of this book for some sources.

Mineral Cups

In your goat shed, you'll also want to mount a pair of mineral cups. One cup will be for minerals and the other will be for baking soda. You'd think you could just nail up two sturdy yogurt containers, but goats have nothing but time and will use that time to destroy their mineral cups if they notice you've scrimped and not given them the real thing. Feed stores sell mineral cups with two compartments. Each compartment

Mineral cups

is about 3 inches deep and 4 inches long and wide. They are made of a thick rubber that even determined goats cannot destroy. Goats are also quite fussy about their minerals being fresh, so add only a few tablespoons at a time and refresh them regularly. If you pour in too much and they don't eat it right away, they probably never will. You'll want to keep your mineral feeder inside the goat shed, where it can be protected from rain and is accessible to the goats at all times. Put it higher than the height of your goats' bottoms (so they don't poop in it) but within easy reach for eating.

Bedding

It is important to keep the floor of your goat shed dry. This is easier said than done, because your goats are going to be continually peeing in the shed. For this reason, it's a good idea to have a wood floor that can drain

You can make an effective and very large compost bin out of old pallets and chicken wire or hardware cloth.

DEEP BEDDING, RICH COMPOST

A popular bedding system among Seattle's urban goat keepers is the deep bedding system. With this system, you lay down about 5 inches of wood shavings. Feed stores sell these shavings in highly compressed cubes encased in plastic. You'll want white shavings or pine shavings, not cedar shavings (which won't compost very well). This first layer of bedding will do its urine absorption job for a few weeks, but then you will begin to detect an ammonia smell. As soon as you do, add another few inches of shavings on top of your original layer. As time goes by, you'll need to add new shavings less and less frequently, because as the bedding gets deeper, it absorbs urine more thoroughly. After about six months, it will be time to dig everything out and place it in a compost pile or compost bin. You will need a big compost bin (about a cubic yard). If you have room for a giant pile, that will do. Alternatively, you can make a large compost bin out of wooden pallets. Moisten the bedding as your pile grows. To optimize the composting action, you'll want the bedding to be as wet as a wrung-out sponge.

It is possible to use straw as bedding in the goat shed, and I often use the stems from alfalfa, which the goats have no interest in and of which I have large quantities. However, straw and alfalfa stems get all matted together and require removal using a pitchfork. They also seem to take longer to compost into something that you can use in your garden.

Before using your goat poop–wood shaving compost on your vegetable bed, you must wait a full year from the date you removed it from the goat shed. This prevents the possible spread of *E. coli* and is of special importance if you plan on using the compost in your vegetable garden. Goat poop alone (not combined with wood shavings) can be used with great success in an ornamental garden. You just don't want to eat any leaves that have touched fresh goat poop, just in case that poop is harboring disease.

moisture (for more on floor drainage, see "Shed Structure and Size" at the beginning of this chapter). To manage the problem of goat pee and poop, you can sweep your goat shed every morning and evening. However, on rainy days when the goats spend most of their day in the shed, they'll end up living in a shallow puddle of their own urine. This is where bedding comes in. Bedding is a layer of wood shavings or straw that covers the entire floor of the goat shed. It absorbs urine, making the shed a more pleasant place to spend time.

Molly snacks on grape leaves, speeding up their transformation into compost.

CHAPTER SEVEN

GOAT DIET AND EXERCISE

GREGORY, THE TERRIBLE EATER IS A CHILDREN'S BOOK intended to help the parents of toddlers who are picky eaters. Gregory is a little goat who won't eat "the usual goat diet" of cardboard boxes and tin cans. The main plot of the story centers around how Gregory's parents manage to coax him into eating a better goat diet. While entertaining and perhaps useful to parents of picky eaters, *Gregory, the Terrible Eater* is based upon the extremely prevalent but also wildly false idea that goats will eat anything. Goats do have a very strange diet when compared with that of humans, but they are, in reality, fussy eaters.

To illustrate how fussy goats can be, I will risk incriminating myself by telling the story of how they drove me into a mild form of thievery. The problem began when, for a period of several days, I gave Snowflake and Brownie maple leaves from a tree some neighbors had recently taken down. When the leaves ran out and I went back to giving them their usual blackberry bramble, they looked at it, gave me a hostile look of appraisal, and then wandered off, refusing to eat. They wouldn't touch their hay either. This went on for a day or two until, getting worried about their health, I drove around my neighborhood and got them more maple leaves.

This, of course, made things worse, and so I spent my entire summer and fall sneaking around and trimming low-level maple branches, telling myself that the maples I stole from really needed trimming anyway. The problem did not get resolved until the fall, when all the maple leaves turned brown and fell from the trees. Snowflake and Brownie did go back to eating blackberry leaves, but it took a few weeks of continually offering fresh branches.

Another myth about goats, mentioned earlier, is that they will mow your lawn. Goats will nibble at grass here and there, but without much enthusiasm, unless the grass is a foot or more tall. If you want an animal to mow your lawn, you will need to get cattle or sheep. Goats are sloppy in their lawn mowing because they are primarily browsers, not grazers. As such, they eat bushes and trees, not grass. The Greeks have an expression for this: "Goats look up and sheep look down."

Although goats will sometimes turn up their noses at what appears to be perfectly acceptable hay, they can also happily dig into many a poisonous plant. Folk wisdom purports that goats begin eating new foods tentatively—taking just a few nibbles at first. It's said that if they then get sick, they won't touch that food again. Folk wisdom is wrong. My friend Alice, having just moved into a new house, had not yet had a chance to ensure that her fence was 100 percent goat-proof. She came home one day to find that her small herd had escaped from the goat yard and eaten her azaleas. They stood on her back porch looking glum and periodically shaking their heads, slinging vomit far and wide. Fortunately, she was able to save them. But two weeks later, she came home to find they'd done it again. She fixed her fence and learned from her mistake that you cannot count on goats to learn from their mistakes.

A goat's diet should be made up of two main types of food—**roughage** and **concentrate.** Roughage refers to green leaves, such as blackberry leaves or the leafy part of a blade of grass, whether it is fresh or dry in the form of hay. Roughage should be available to your goats at all times and should make up the majority of their diet. Concentrate refers to a richer food source, primarily grain with a protein supplement. Purina Mills Goat Chow is an example of a concentrate. Concentrate should be given to goats in relatively small amounts, with the amount varying according to whether they are pregnant, where they are in their pregnancy, and how much milk they are giving. If your goat is not pregnant and not lactating, you should not feed her any concentrate. In addition to roughage and concentrate, your goat will require a goat-specific loose **mineral mix** to be available at all times.

Roughage

Roughage is an extremely important part of your goats' diet, and by volume, it is by far the largest component of their diet. Roughage can be hay or the fresh leaves of various plants. A portion of a goat's roughage can be given in pelletized form (alfalfa pellets).

When you first go to a feed store to buy hay, and they ask you, "What kind of hay would you like?" it is important that you not say, "Oh, just regular hay will be fine." It turns out that there is an amazing variety of hay out there, that the differences between

THE RUMBLING RUMEN: A SIGN OF GOOD HEALTH

Goats have four stomachs: the rumen, reticulum, omasum, and abomasum. They work quite differently from yours and mine. The primary stomach is called a rumen, and it is a giant fermentation vat in which bacteria break down the nutrients of the leaves, grass, and bark that a goat consumes. The goat in turn digests the by-products of the bacteria. From the rumen, the first stomach of the goat's digestive system, partially digested food goes into either the reticulum (if it needs further mechanical breaking down) or the omasum (if it doesn't). The reticulum sends the food in need of further chewing (the cud) back up through the esophagus to the mouth. The goat then chews it some more before swallowing it a second time, thereby sending it back to the rumen. Eventually, the food enters the fourth and only "true" stomach of the goat, the abomasum. From there, it travels through the intestines and is absorbed as energy and nutrients. The remaining debris gets ejected in the form of tidy pellets, which as a goat owner, you will come to know well.

The important thing to remember in the confusion of all these stomachs and cud chewing is that the millions and millions of microscopic bacteria in the stomachs of a goat are critical. Without them, the goat could not break down into a digestible form high-fiber foods like leaves, grass, and bark.

Given the low number of calories in grass and leaves, goats need to eat a tremendous volume of this material, and their rumen is almost always at work, gurgling and burping away. When you first bring your goat home, press your ear to her left side and try to listen for rumblings. Do this often to get a sense of what a healthy rumen sounds like. If your goat is acting a bit listless or she seems off her food, listen to her rumen. If you listen for a minute and hear fewer than three rumbles, she's sick and you'll need to get help quickly. Do not wait even a single day. A goat cannot survive long without a healthy rumen.

all the varieties are important, and that if you confuse hay with straw, you might just starve your goats. Here is what you need to know about hay before visiting a feed store.

ALFALFA

Alfalfa is the number one roughage fed to animals, and unlike timothy and orchard grass, alfalfa is not a grass—it is a legume. It looks a lot like clover but can reach 3 feet tall. Alfalfa is highly nutritious—with the highest protein and calcium levels of all the hays. Alfalfa hay is in many ways the perfect feed for goats who are pregnant or lactating or still under a year old and growing fast. It is rich in energy, nutrients, and long fiber. It is not, however, the perfect feed for goats who are dry, not growing, and not pregnant. If you feed one of these nonpregnant, nonlactating, and nongrowing goats alfalfa in any significant quantity, she will get fat. Alfalfa is a little bit like walnuts. It is extremely nutritious but also extremely rich in calories, which is good if you need the calories, but bad if you don't.

There is another problem with alfalfa related to the upkeep of your goat yard. Alfalfa is made of fibrous stems, which contain little nutrition, and of leaves, which are green, rich in nutrients, and rich in calories. Your goats will *love* the alfalfa leaves and spend many hours of their day pulling large clumps of alfalfa out from the feeder, nibbling off the leaves, and dropping large piles of stems on the ground. This means you will end up with a huge amount of worthless stems, and your compost bins will be overflowing.

As a solution to this problem, there are alfalfa pellets. These are made from alfalfa that has been carefully ground up and compressed into pellets. These pellets have the same nutritional benefits as alfalfa in hay form, but the goats can't do as much picking

Alfalfa is made up of fibrous stems and leaves that are rich in calories, vitamins, and minerals. *(Photo from istockphoto.com)*

and sorting through them, so much less is wasted. However, the fibers in alfalfa pellets are not long enough to ensure the health of the goat's long and complicated digestive tract. To correct this problem, you'll also want to feed second-cutting orchard grass (see below).

One last issue with alfalfa is that all bales of alfalfa are not equal. Often, first- and second-cutting alfalfa is made up mostly of worthless stems. Third- and fourth-cutting alfalfa tends to be made up primarily of green leaves. The kind of alfalfa you want is third and fourth cutting. Sadly, these are often available only at certain times of the year. If no good alfalfa is available, go with the pellets and use some other type of hay, such as orchard grass or timothy.

ORCHARD GRASS

Orchard grass is an actual grass. It consists of long, thin grass leaves with very thin stems. This means that goats can't pick off their favorite green leafy section. Since they won't be able to pick the leaves off the stems, you will have far fewer stems piling

Goats are primarily browsers, meaning they prefer food at eye level or above, like bushes. In contrast, sheep are grazers who eat food that's below their eye level, like grass.

up under your hay manger. Orchard grass has the long fibers that goats need. While orchard grass is an excellent hay in terms of fiber, it doesn't have the protein or calcium necessary for pregnant or lactating goats. That is why you should always have alfalfa pellets available if your goats are pregnant or lactating and you are feeding orchard grass. Second-cutting orchard grass is preferable to first cutting in terms of the ratio of nutritious leaf to stem and stalk.

TIMOTHY GRASS
Timothy can be used instead of orchard grass. If orchard grass and timothy are both available, compare the two by examining their ratio of stem to leaf. You want lots of leaf and not much stem. Generally, however, orchard grass is preferable to timothy.

STRAW
Straw is what is left over from the harvesting of grains. It is pure stem and has almost no nutritional value to goats. It can be used for bedding, but must never be used as a feed.

IMPORTANT NOTE: KEEP IT FRESH!
While hay is a key component of a goat's diet, goats do not like hay that has sat in their feeder for more than a day or two. Perhaps their eyes or noses can detect a thin layer of dust that is beyond the ability of humans to perceive. Whatever the reason, most goats will not eat hay that's been in their feeder for more than 48 hours.

FORAGING FOR YOUR GOAT
Although in theory it is possible for goats to live on good-quality dried hay and alfalfa pellets, fresh leaves, especially the bright young green leaves of spring, are extremely good for them. Some people manage to collect fresh forage (browse) year round for their goats. Others do so only occasionally. Sometimes in the spring, you will *need* to

WHERE TO FIND HAY

In general, feed stores are the best places from which to buy hay, as they often have a variety of types from which to choose. Feed stores also have buyers who check hay for quality, and generally, these buyers do a fairly good job. If you have contacts in the farming world, you may be able to hook up with a farmer and buy your hay direct. However, learning to tell good hay from bad takes time, so it's best to buy from a reputable feed store until you are sure you know what you are doing.

forage for your goats. It is in the spring that you'll find yourself with a voracious goat and an empty hay box. This is because goats typically give birth in the spring, so during this time of year they'll either be in the last stages of their pregnancy or feeding one to three kids. And, because good-quality hay is harvested in the late summer and early fall, it is often sold out by spring. The upside to this problem is that spring is the time when opportunities for foraging are at their best and many leaves are highest in nutrients.

There are a wide variety of plants that your goats will enjoy and that will help put them in top form. You can't buy these at a feed store, but in most places you should be able to step outside and find some free for the taking. Good plants for goat forage include:

- Blackberries
- Fresh grass (tall varieties)
- Clover
- Dandelions
- Kudzu
- Apple leaves
- Maple leaves
- Roses (hips, leaves, and flowers)
- Fresh vegetables, especially carrots (but *not* potato tops or tomato plants)

The mainstay of my goats' diet is blackberry. All up and down the west coast, from San Diego to Seattle, nonnative Himalayan blackberry bushes burst forth with new growth and invasive vigor in early spring, and if you head out with your clippers, welder's gloves, and a canvas log carrier, you will be popular with both your neighbors and your goats. I have *never* had anyone complain about my pruning their blackberry bushes, and I do it almost every day in the spring and summer.

While blackberry leaves are typically free for the taking, they are also extremely nutritious. New spring blackberry leaves contain 21 percent protein, more than is in alfalfa. They also contain 0.91 percent calcium, a relatively high amount (but not as much as is found in alfalfa, 1.15 percent). The downside to blackberries is the thorny canes that the goats don't eat. These are a nuisance to haul out of your goat yard and cram into a yard waste bin.

Goats also enjoy fresh grass, clover, and dandelion. To collect these, you need to find a vacant lot or the edge of a park that has not been mowed. If you live in a neighborhood where all the gardens are perfectly manicured, you'll have to venture forth into the neighborhoods of your city where the gardens run wilder. Whatever you do, make sure your goats do not eat grass cuttings that have begun to break down anaerobically. This can cause serious illness.

In certain parts of the United States, other nonnatives grow that are said to be nutritious and popular with goats. The South has kudzu. The Southwest has buffelgrass (*Pennisetum ciliare*), an invasive grass originally planted as forage for cattle.

There are many other plants that you can forage for your goats—apple leaves, maple leaves, salal, rosebush—but if you were to harvest these about town without permission, you'd probably find yourself in trouble. And many of the plants common in urban areas are poisonous to goats—laurel, rhododendron, and azaleas being especially dangerous. For this reason, it's important to review the partial list of poisonous plants that follows and make sure that what you are giving your goat is not on it. For a complete list of common poisonous plants in North America, check Cornell University's website (www.ansci.cornell.edu/plants/). Cornell's list is thorough but not ideal, as it doesn't distinguish between plants that could simply upset your goat's stomach and those that could kill your goat quickly.

Here is a list of some of the **most common poisonous plants to avoid:**

- Azalea
- Buttercup
- Bracken fern
- Cherry tree
- Common milkweed
- Daphne
- Elderberry
- Foxglove
- Hemlock
- Lantana
- Laurel
- Lily of the valley
- Locoweed
- Lupine
- Oak tree
- Plum tree
- Poison ivy
- Pokeweed
- Poppy
- Potato
- Rhododendron
- Rhubarb
- Spurge
- St. John's Wort
- Tobacco
- Wisteria
- Yew

You might think to yourself that going out and collecting forage for your goats is a foolish idea when you could just bring your goat to the forage and save yourself some trouble. In fact, before I brought my goats home, I had visions of tethering them to a tree in the woods near my house to have them help clear the land of invasive nonnatives. However, once I had the goats in my yard and was ready to set out, it occurred to me that I would need to sit with them while they ate to protect them from any marauding dogs or from getting cords tangled around their necks. I soon realized that going foraging with my goats would eat up my time.

Goats must eat such a huge volume of roughage to get the calories they need that they must spend an equally huge amount of time eating. In an article titled "Selective Behaviour of Goats Offered Different Tropical Foliages," Kongmanila Daovy, T. R. Preston, and Inger Ledin observed individual goats for eight consecutive days to see how much time they spent eating a variety of foliages. Between 8:00 AM and 5:00 PM, the goats were observed to eat for four hours and twenty minutes. This means they spent a full 48 percent of those daytime hours eating! In another study conducted by researchers B.M. Domingue, D.W. Dellow, and T.N. Barry in New Zealand, goats were observed to spend seven hours of a twenty-four-hour day eating and another six hours chewing their cud.

It also explains why it is not at all practical for your modern American to take their goats on a walk to a blackberry patch and expect them to eat enough food for the day. Such a walk would take all day, given that goats need to rest between their nibbling and chew their cud before moving on to nibble some more.

MESSY EATERS NEED HELP: FOLIAGE FEEDERS

I have often heard it said that goats are extremely wasteful, as if their tendency to grab huge clumps of hay and then drop large parts of those clumps onto the floor were due to some sort of character flaw. While goats do eat this way, and it is a nuisance, it is not because they are intrinsically wasteful or slothful. As browsers, they evolved to pull leaves from a tree and munch away. If you watch a goat eating from a tree, you will notice that there is no waste. The problem comes about when, in grabbing hay, more hay than they meant to take comes out. Modern hay feeders are just not designed quite like trees.

The goat eating method is particularly a problem when you bring them bundles of browse. If you put the browse in a box, your goats will pull out a whole stem, nibble a few leaves, and drop the stem and the remaining leaves onto the ground. In general, once something falls onto the ground and gets stepped on, a goat will not eat it. In this

YOU ARE WHAT YOUR GOAT EATS

While foraging for your goat will help make her happy and healthy, it will make you healthy too (if not happy; clipping blackberries is not that fun, although it is sort of gratifying). Wild plants, such as blackberry and kudzu, are often extremely rich in nutrients. In addition, because goats are primarily browsers, the leaves of fresh plants are generally healthier for them than the small leaves of dried grass hay or even alfalfa. By feeding your goat the food she evolved to eat, you'll be keeping her in top condition. In turn, her milk should be nutritionally far superior to the milk of a factory-farmed goat (and yes, there is such a thing).

way, goats are fastidious. This habit prevents goats from contracting a host of diseases that can be passed through eating food contaminated with fecal matter.

To deal with the problem of feeding branches with leaves to goats, use a foliage feeder, as discussed in Chapter 5. A foliage feeder is easy to build and will save you and your goats time and energy.

Concentrate

Many dairy goats, at the peak of their lactation, can easily produce a gallon of milk a day. Assuming that a cup of milk contains approximately 170 calories, a goat at peak lactation is *giving* about 2,700 calories a day. Even if you give your goat the finest-quality roughage available, and she has it available at all times (and you should be doing this), she will not be able to get enough calories with roughage alone to continue at that level of milk production. In addition, she would rapidly become dangerously thin.

For this reason, when your goat is lactating, you need to supplement her diet with what dairy farmers call a concentrate. Goat chow is a concentrate made of grain, vitamin supplements, and some type of high-protein meal, such as soy meal. Sometimes it comes as a loose, crumbly mixture; sometimes it comes in pelletized form; and sometimes it's a combination of the two.

WHAT TYPE OF CONCENTRATE TO FEED

My favorite goat vet recommends feeding commercial goat feed concentrates such as Purina Mills Goat Chow or Nutrena Top Goat. (Note: Purina Mills, the company that makes Purina Mills Goat Chow, is not to be confused with Purina, the company that makes dog and cat food. The two companies were divided many years ago.) My vet recommends Purina Mills and Nutrena because he reasons that they have carefully researched goat nutrition needs and come up with a well-balanced option. In recent years, several small companies have begun to develop organic lines of goat feed. These can also be quite good, and some are no doubt better.

Some people develop their own goat concentrates by mixing together a grain, such as corn or oats, with a protein supplement, such as Vigor Plus. This can save money but requires knowledge and expertise. The idea is to end up with a concentrate that contains 16 to 18 percent protein. If the roughage your goat eats is high in protein, as is the case with alfalfa and blackberry leaves, you'll want to a concentrate with a protein level of 13 percent. If you want to lower the protein level of a commercial concentrate, you can mix in COB (a combination of corn, oats, and barley). The labels on goat chow and COB tell you the percent protein they contain; you'll need to mix accordingly.

WHEN TO START AND HOW MUCH TO FEED

You need to begin giving concentrate to your goat on about the ninetieth day of her pregnancy. This is the point at which the kids within her begin their growth spurt. When you introduce the concentrate, give just ½ cup in the morning and ½ cup at night. Over the period of a week, slowly increase the amount you are giving her to 1 cup every morning and night. Continue to give her this amount until she kids. Once she kids, you will need to increase the amount of concentrate you feed even more.

The amount of concentrate you need to feed your newly lactating doe will depend in part on your goat. Some goats have better rumens that can take in more roughage than others. It will also depend on how much and what type of browse you bring your goat.

There is a wide range of advice on the amount of concentrate to feed your goat. I like a ratio of 1 pound of concentrate per 3 pounds (6 cups) of milk, because I found some actual data to back it up. Bruce Clement, of the University of New Hampshire Cooperative Extension in Durham, New Hampshire, worked with several goat farmers and divided their herds into three groups. One group got 1 pound of concentrate a day, one got 3 pounds a day, and one got 5 pounds a day. They also tracked how much milk each goat gave per day. Their results showed that to maximize production and herd health, the optimum ratio was 1 pound of concentrate to 3 pounds of milk.

To convert the 1 pound of concentrate to 3 pounds of milk rule into a volume-based rule, you can assume that milk weighs ½ pound per cup and that concentrate weighs ¼ pound per cup. This translates to 1 cup of concentrate per 1½ cups of milk.

Feeding goats more than this amount is not cost-effective, and it can also be very unhealthy for the goat. Too much rich food causes an imbalance in their rumen and can lead to diarrhea and/or enterotoxaemia, an extremely dangerous condition in goats. If you notice that your goat's droppings are beginning to clump together instead of forming neat, individual pellets, you may want to cut back on the amount of concentrate you are feeding. (Such clumping can also be caused by internal parasites. If you cut back on grain and the poops still clump together, you will want to send in a fecal sample for testing.)

After reading about the benefits of grass-fed beef and of milk from grass-fed cows, I have strived to cut back on the amount of concentrate that I feed my goats. Although I've worked hard to feed my newly lactating goats armloads of blackberry bramble each day, they still seem to require the 1-to-3 ratio by weight of concentrate to milk. I know of other people, however, who have succeeded in cutting back their concentrate ratio. I recently learned that my friend Melany gives her goats only 1 cup of grain per day during their entire lactation cycle. These goats give ample amounts of milk and look perfectly healthy. How Melany's goats can do what they do I do not know, but it is worth giving

Melany's system a try, as long as your goat is producing well and is a healthy weight. Melany brings her goat a large amount and a wide variety of fresh browse every day.

When figuring out how much concentrate to feed your goat, remember to include in your calculations the amount of milk that the kids are drinking. Using the system outlined in Chapter 9, you will let the kids spend the day with their mother, drinking as much from her as they like, and then in the evening you will separate them from her for a full twelve hours. They get to join their mother again in the morning, after you have milked her out completely. To figure out how much milk the kids have drunk, you can assume that they are getting just as much as you are milking. Take this amount into your calculations for how much concentrate to feed, and feed her this additional amount in the evening after you've tucked the kids in for the night.

HOW PREGNANCY AND LACTATION CHANGE YOUR GOAT'S DIETARY NEEDS

What you feed your goat during pregnancy is extremely important. She must have the proper ratio of calcium to phosphorus, or she can experience hypocalcaemia (lack of calcium). This can quickly lead to the death of both mother and kids. Calcium is critical for the growth of the kids, and immense amounts are needed during the last two months of a doe's pregnancy, when the kids grow most rapidly. Without enough calcium, your doe's body will begin to take the calcium from her own bones. In addition, in an effort to set right the calcium-to-phosphorus ratio, she'll stop eating her grain and go into a state of ketosis. Should your goat begin to show a loss of interest in her concentrate during the last few months of her pregnancy, get her to the vet right away. She probably has developed hypocalcaemia and, secondarily, ketosis. This can lead to death within a few days.

Although it is extremely important for a doe to have calcium during heavy lactation and during the last two months of her pregnancy, it can't be absorbed without phosphorus, and that ratio of calcium to phosphorus must be 2 to 1. While orchard grass has a perfect 2-to-1 ratio of calcium to phosphorus, it has very little of both. Thus, if you are feeding orchard grass, and then you feed concentrate, which is very rich in phosphorus, the 2-to-1 ratio will be thrown out of whack, and your doe will not be able to absorb the small amount of calcium available in the orchard grass. For this reason, if you are feeding only orchard grass, you must not feed any concentrate. In addition, it's extremely important that you provide alfalfa pellets and have them available to your pregnant goat at all times. If you find that your goat isn't eating them, check to make sure that no poop has gotten in with the pellets and that the pellets are fresh.

FEEDING GUIDELINES FOR A DOE

CONDITION OF DOE	IF YOU ARE FEEDING ORCHARD GRASS	IF YOU ARE FEEDING ALFALFA HAY
Growing doeling (18 weeks to one year)	Always have alfalfa pellets available to the doeling and do not feed concentrate unless you are training and need a simple reward.	Do not feed any concentrate unless you are training and need a simple reward.
Not pregnant, not lactating, and over one year of age	Do not feed any concentrate. Do not feed any alfalfa pellets.	Stop. You should not feed alfalfa or alfalfa pellets to full-grown goats who are not pregnant and not lactating.
Pregnant but not lactating; first three months of pregnancy	Always have alfalfa pellets available to the doe. Do not feed any concentrate.	Feed a total of ½ to 1 cup of concentrate a day. (Feed ½ cup if your doe is on the heavy side and 1 cup if she is on the lean side.) This concentrate is intended to increase her phosphorus intake, since the alfalfa doesn't have enough.
Pregnant and lactating; first three months of pregnancy	Always have alfalfa pellets available to the doe.	At milking time, feed her as much as 2 cups of concentrate for every 3 cups of milk she gives.
Pregnant; last two months of pregnancy (your goat should not be lactating at this time—if she is, dry her off)	If possible, switch to good-quality alfalfa hay. Otherwise, make sure she has access to fresh alfalfa pellets at all times.	Feed 1 cup, but no more than 1 cup, of concentrate every morning and evening.
Lactating but not pregnant	Always have alfalfa pellets available to the doe. At milking time, feed, at a maximum and depending on condition, 2 cups of concentrate for every 3 cups of milk your goat gives.	In the morning and evening, feed her 2 cups of concentrate for every 3 cups of milk she gives.

NOTE: Even if you are feeding alfalfa hay, it is a good idea to make alfalfa pellets available at all times. Sometimes your goats will eat the alfalfa stems clean, and the pellets are good to have as a backup food source.

As I mentioned earlier, alfalfa pellets alone do not provide adequate fiber length for goats, so they cannot substitute for hay on their own.

Do remember that the information in the table is meant simply as a guideline. If your goat's poop begins to clump together, cut back slightly on the concentrate and make sure she has baking soda in one of her mineral cups. If she is too fat, again you'll want to cut back on her concentrate. Of course, this takes us to a tricky question—how can you tell if your goat is fat? It's not that easy.

Many people lack diplomacy and manners, and upon seeing a goat with a healthy rumen will comment on how fat she is. Calmly point out to these people that if they had four stomachs, they'd look fat too. You can't go by the size of your goat's stomach as an indication of her condition. Look at her neck and her ribs. Feel her spine. To learn a healthy weight for goats, go visit the goats at summer fairs, talk to goat owners, and look at and touch as many goats as you can. It's important to be able to tell when your goat is a healthy weight.

Minerals

When looking for a mineral supplement for goats, make sure you do not buy anything made for both sheep and goats. While copper can poison a sheep, goats require it. Thus, a sheep and goat mineral mix will almost ensure that your goat will experience a copper deficiency. You might think that a goat who eats a healthy diet of browse would be getting all the minerals she needs. Sadly, this is not the case. The nutrients of plants often depend heavily on the nutrients of the soil within which they grow. The soil in some parts of our country is low in certain minerals. For example, much of the soil in the Northwest is low in copper, so no matter how careful you are to ensure that your goat gets lots of lush green browse, she will still be copper deficient without a mineral supplement containing copper, and this deficiency can wreak havoc on her physiology. For this reason, loose goat minerals must be available to goats at all times. Two mineral brands that are popular among goat keepers are Sweetlix Meat Maker for goats (the nonmedicated variety) and Golden Blend Goat Minerals. In addition, if the minerals sit for a few weeks in their dish, you'll need to throw them away and add new minerals. Goats will not touch what they consider to be stale minerals. This is just the frustrating nature of goats.

You will often hear people say that goats know what they need and will eat their minerals accordingly, but this is true only for salt. Goats will eat their minerals until they have had enough salt, and then stop. The best minerals for goats take this into account.

Baking Soda

Baking soda helps reduce the acidity of a goat's rumen, and they will nibble at it on an as-needed basis. It is especially important to have baking soda available to your goats at all times if they are lactating heavily and eating relatively large amounts of concentrate.

Thirty Minutes of Aerobic Exercise Each Day

My friend Anna had a goat who had trouble "self-regulating" her eating, and her vet told her she'd have to give the goat thirty minutes of cardio exercise each day. Technically, Seattle's goat law specifies that you can walk goats only for "transportation purposes." So even in goat-friendly Seattle, you are supposed to walk your goat only if you need to take her someplace. While this severely cramps my goats' style, there is a good reason for it. The problem with walking a goat in the city is that their poop, while not gross or smelly, and excellent manure for the garden, can spread disease, just as any other poop can. You might think, "But dogs poop and you can just pooper scoop it up." This makes sense until you have tried walking a goat around your neighborhood. Goats poop about eight times more frequently than dogs do, and they let out a whole stream of berries that bounce far and wide. Collecting them all is a tricky business.

However, after five years of owning goats in the city, I've come to think that they need exercise just as much as dogs and people do. This does not mean you have to take your goats jogging, but it is a good idea to get them out walking for about thirty minutes a few days a week. To do this, you will need what are called bun bags or berry bags. (See the Goaty Resources section at the end of the book for a source.)

You will also need to get your goats used to walking in the city. This you can do simply by taking them for walks every day. If you purchase your goats when they are kids, begin practicing public leash walks right away. You can use leashes and adjustable harnesses made for dogs. Early on, your goats will be spooked by cars, bikes, and dogs and may try to bolt. This is why it's a good idea to train them young. Hanging onto a 100-pound goat dead set on running as fast as she possibly can

This goat is obese. You can tell by looking at her chest. A large pot belly does not necessarily mean that your goat is fat.

Eloise always enjoys stepping out. Without a bun bag, pooper scooping can be a challenge. On these stairs, the pellets bounce down, down, and all around.

is difficult and unpleasant work. This problem is compounded by the need to walk your goats together. Goats, being herd animals, are often so bonded to one another that they just won't walk without their companion with them. This means that you may have to walk both your goats at the same time. Two spooked 100-pound goats could easily pull you over and drag you down the street. If you can teach your goats to behave on a leash when they are small, you just may be able to safely take both of them for walks by your-self when they reach full size.

Some goat owners have trained their goats to walk calmly at their sides through clicker training. The clicker helps the animals connect the behavior they are being rewarded for with their treat. The moment the goat does what you want her to do, you click, and you follow this up with a reward within 30 seconds. You can just say "good," but the consistency of the clicker sound has been shown to triple the speed of training. The clicker method is a favorite among Hollywood's animal movie-star trainers. To train your goat to walk calmly at your side using the clicker method, you must first train her to touch her nose to a target. In this case, your target is a rubber ball or KONG dog toy attached to a 2-foot-long stick. When the goat touches the rubber end of the stick, you click and give her a treat.

Once your goat has mastered the art of touching the target with her nose, you can lure her to walk calmly next to you as you hold the target in front of her. Begin with hav-ing her take a single step before hitting the target. Then slowly increase the number of steps she takes. After a time, when she begins to walk, give her a new command, such as "Heel." Once she connects this command with walking at your side, you can leave the target at home. (See Goaty Resources at the end of the book for sources of more infor-mation on clicker training.) Note: When teaching your goat tricks, it's best to start in your own goat yard, where she feels comfortable and is used to its distractions.

For treats, air-popped popcorn works well, since it is high in volume and low in calories, and goats like it. You can also use a teaspoon of goat concentrate, peanuts in the shell, a few sunflower seeds, or small slices of carrots or apple.

If you are concerned that a dog might attack while you are walking, a marine horn can be helpful. Sold at marine supply stores, these are cans of highly compressed air that let out an ear-splitting noise when you press the trigger. They are quite effective at stopping an attack.

This youngster peeks through a hole in her goat shed as a distant voice croons, "Doeling, you'll be a dairy doe soon."

CHAPTER EIGHT

FROM DOELING TO DAIRY GOAT

MOST PEOPLE BEGIN THEIR GOAT KEEPING WITH TWO DOELINGS. Doelings are ready to leave their mother at eight weeks old. They will cry for the first few days because they will miss their mother and their herd. But after that they should settle down and come to appreciate their new surroundings, and peace will be restored. Because new kids can be so noisy, it is a good idea to let your neighbors know what is happening and that the crying shouldn't continue for more than a few days. Dam-raised goats are able to leave their mothers at eight weeks old. From eight weeks on, they have no need of their mother's milk and will get by very nicely on hay, pasture, and browse.

Transporting eight-week-old kids is relatively easy due to their small size. A large dog crate with straw or wood shavings in the bottom can hold two young kids comfortably. Goat pee has a way of getting loose from the crate, even when you have straw or wood shavings in the bottom, so it's wise to put a tarp under the crate to keep your car from smelling like goat pee for a very long time.

Raising Kids

Having a pair of baby goats is incredibly fun, and upon getting to know them, you'll stop wondering how the word *kid* began to be applied to human children. Both human and goat kids love to jump and run and race around. When they aren't busy with this sort of cardiorespiratory workout, they are busy eating, and when they aren't busy eating, they can be found sleeping. While they sometimes curl up in a corner by themselves to catch a few Zs, they prefer to nestle next to their mother or sibling. They also enjoy napping on human laps and having their backs stroked.

During their first year of life, goats grow exponentially. Because they are growing so quickly, they'll need calcium. For the first year, you'll want to feed them a combination of orchard grass and alfalfa pellets, or you can simply feed alfalfa hay. Growing goats do not need any concentrate during their first year, but it's okay to give them a quarter cup as a treat now and again, especially if it is for training purposes.

Given the problem that noisy goats can cause, it's important to make sure that you don't accidentally train your goats to be noisy by going out and giving them loving pats to calm them down whenever they get noisy. Visit them only when they are being quiet and are on their best behavior. See the "Noisy Goats" section in Chapter 3 for more information on minimizing the noise made by goats.

When Your Doeling Becomes a Doe

If your goat was born in the early summer, she won't reach breeding age (ten months) until after breeding season is over. (Breeding season generally runs from September through February and varies by region and goat.) If this is the case, you'll have to wait until mating season begins again in the fall for her to breed. If you find all this waiting difficult, remember that the time between your purchase of your doeling and when you breed her is a great time to settle into goat ownership, bond with your goat, and work out any kinks in your system and setup. You may discover that your spigot is too far from the bucket or that your hay box leaks. If you are going to be doing your own hoof trimming, this is the time to practice. It is much easier to trim the hooves of a goat that is only three months old than it is to trim those of a hundred-pounder.

Does have an estrus cycle of approximately twenty-one days, and their heats last between twelve and forty-eight hours. So even before you breed your doe, see if you can tell when she goes into heat. This will help you figure out when she is likely to come into heat again.

Sometimes it is very obvious when a doe is in heat. After having had my goats Snowflake and Brownie for only a few months, I woke up one morning to Brownie yelling up a storm. I ran down to see if she was okay, and nothing looked wrong. I then headed out to walk the dog and was considering how to best transport Brownie to the vet when a neighbor looked up from taking out her trash and asked, "Is one of your goats in heat?" I knew at once that she'd hit the nail on the head. She's from New York City, so how she figured out what was going on is still a mystery to me. In any event, she was right and this crying, or calling really, lasted for several days, and lots of people asked whether my goats were okay. I explained that Brownie was just calling out into the wilds of the city in search of a mate. Fortunately, she did not do this again for another twenty-one days, and as the year progressed she got quieter with each successive heat.

Sometimes estrus is less obvious. A few years back, when I was ready to breed Brownie, she was silent. To tell if she had come into heat, I had to get a buck rag (a rag that has been rubbed all over a male goat). Each day I would show it to Brownie, and she'd give it a look, and sometimes a nibble, but in general she didn't find it any more interesting than a regular rag. This continued for several days until one day, upon seeing the rag, she wagged her tail madly. The rag clearly had come to mean more to her. It enthralled her, and all she wanted was to be near it and nuzzle it. That evening, I whisked her off to the stud buck, Valentino, and sure enough, the time was right.

When it's not so obvious whether your doe is in heat, here are some signs to look for:

- Tail flagging. Her tail will flick back and forth quickly. She won't just flag a few times; she'll do it a lot.
- Vocalizing more frequently than usual.
- The area just outside the vagina may turn pinker than the surrounding flesh.
- A drop of mucus may hang from her vagina or dry up and become attached to her tail.
- Being mounted by or mounting a companion goat (even if the companion is the same sex or a neutered male).

Some does show all of these signs, and some show very few of them. Some show them even when they aren't really in heat. So telling whether your goat is in heat can be tricky. A checklist with an area for comments can be a big help. If your doe's heats

CHECKLIST TO HELP IDENTIFY WHEN YOUR GOAT IS IN ESTRUS

- How many times does she flag over a period of 60 seconds?
- Does she pee within 10 seconds of smelling the buck rag?
- What is the color surrounding the area just outside her vagina?
- Are there signs of vaginal discharge (dried bits of goop stuck to her tail)?
- Have you heard her bleating from the house? If yes, how often?
- Have you heard her bleating while you've been with her in the goat yard?
- Have you noticed your goat engaging in any unusual behavior, such as mounting or being mounted by her goat companion?

aren't obvious, try recording how she reacts to a buck rag over a twenty-one day period, to get a sense of how she responds over the course of her cycle.

As noted, buck rags have a very strong smell and should be stored in a screw-top jar to preserve their odor and to prevent everything around them from picking up the odor. You may wonder, "But where does one buy a buck rag? I have never in my life seen one for sale." Buck rags are a specialty item, and you get them from the owner of the buck who you plan to use as the stud buck for your doe.

EVEN EDUCATED FLEAS DO IT

Your doeling should be at least ten months old before being bred. You will find several books that say it is fine to breed a standard dairy goat as young as seven months old, but this can be risky. I know goat owners who have had some bad experiences with breeding goats this young—the kids, the mother, or both died at the time of birth. Also,

Like most stud bucks, Morgan gets a crazy look in his eye during rutting season.

if you look at a seven-month-old doeling, she doesn't look fully mature and it simply doesn't seem right to breed so young.

Unneutered male goats (bucks) are not allowed under many city codes, including Seattle. This is no problem. When one of my does goes into heat, I just pop her into the back of my station wagon and take her to a stud buck for a $75 fee. This is what I would do even if bucks were allowed in the city. It would cost much more than $75 to feed a buck for a year. Also, given their unsavory personalities, stud bucks will ruin the wholesome atmosphere of your goat garden room.

Usually, when you take your doe to the stud buck, you will put her in a smallish pen together with the stud buck, and you and the buck owner will stand outside the pen and wait for them to mate a total of three times. After the third time, sperm numbers drop to the point that an additional mating won't increase your goat's chance of pregnancy. If your goat mates only once or twice, that's okay, but mating three times gives you the best chance of your goat "settling" (becoming pregnant).

THE THIRD TIME'S THE CHARM

You might think, "Three times! I haven't got that much time." Do not worry. Amazingly, goats are very quick in their mating, and your doe and her stud buck will probably finish their three matings within half an hour. The rapidity of goat mating and their virility is truly remarkable. A goat farmer I know from the farmers' market told me that one of his does once brushed briefly past one of his bucks when he was moving his herd around and poof, she was pregnant. It literally takes goats only seconds to mate. This is because they are prey animals. There's just no time for them to mess around. When I heard this, I wondered about lions. It turns out that female lions do not even have a regular estrus cycle. They go into heat only after mating about a hundred times. Thus, when lions are ready to breed, they must do so with gusto. They mate every fifteen to twenty minutes for two to three days (two hundred to three hundred times). And what of hamsters, the ultimate prey animal? They go into heat every four days.

If you make a mistake regarding your goat being in heat, you'll find out as soon as you put her together with the stud buck. Does are interested in mating only if they are in heat. If they aren't in heat, they will snub the stud buck, refusing to give him the time of day.

While chances are good that your goat will settle if all has proceeded according to plan with her stud buck date, there is still the possibility that she won't. This is

NO POPPING

One morning, when it was around the time of year to bring Snowflake in for a rendez-vous with her stud buck, I showed her the buck rag, and she clearly got excited to see it. She was flagging like crazy, and she stood at the top of the stairs yelling, despite the rain. She must have known that her man was miles away because she was pretty loud. She was in heat.

I had always been kind of flippant in the past about how easy it is to pop a goat in the back of a station wagon and take her to a buck. I think this cavalier attitude must have brought on some sort of bad juju, because there was no "popping" of goats this time.

The first trouble was that I had no station wagon. Don had taken it to work and left me with our old Volvo 240 sedan. I love this old bomber, but it is not so good for haul-ing goats. I decided to make do and loaded Snowflake into an extra-large dog crate. The trouble was that I wasn't strong enough to lift the large crate and 100-pound goat into the trunk of the car. I went to get my next-door neighbor to get help, but after a few attempts, she said we would hurt our backs and that she'd go see if she could find her hunky husband. She always calls him that, "my hunky husband," which might seem odd, but if you saw her husband, you'd understand. Anyway, the hunky husband wasn't around, so she and I went knocking on all the other neighbors' doors, but they must have seen us coming or were off being gainfully employed, because no one answered.

Next, I turned to my farm boy, Spencer, for help. He's nine and had his sidekick Bryce over, and they were busy building a Lego fortress that they planned to destroy later with Spencer's super-huge Nerf arsenal. Despite being deeply involved in this project, the idea of lifting a goat captured their interest, and they came out to help me. And as it turned out, those two little nine-year-olds and I managed to get the crate into the trunk. It was really hard and involved a lot of stages, such as balancing the crate on the fender, but we managed to get it up and in without dropping or hurt-ing Snowflake.

The next hurdle was getting Bryce and Spencer to agree to go with me. Spencer is a painfully good negotiator. He always aims high and never takes no as a final answer, and he and Bryce really did not want to drive 45 minutes to a farm when they could be playing with Legos and shooting Nerf guns. So after some major haggling involving unhealthy snacks and a movie, they agreed to come along. Sometimes I negotiate with terrorists.

Next we were delayed because I had to put together the unhealthy snack, and they had to find a very specific Lego-monsters-at-war comic book, but we finally all got buckled up.

Now comes the really sad part. When I went to put the key in the ignition, there was no ignition. When I looked down at my feet, I saw a pile of metal shavings. Turns out someone had tried to steal my car the night before, but had gotten spooked and run off. Without an ignition, I could not start the car.

We unloaded Snowflake from the car, and I reported the incident to the police. The upside of all this was that Spencer and Bryce had a very happy day. They managed to enjoy the unhealthy snack while I was distracted, they didn't have to go anywhere, and a really nice policeman came to the door and admired their accuracy with Nerf guns. I felt low, though—no pregnant goat and a big car repair bill. And Snowflake? She was heartbroken.

the nature of the sperm and egg and the challenges they face in getting together. If a mating doesn't take, two things can happen. First, she may bounce. In the bounce scenario, she will come back into heat four to seven days after her mating. Second, she may come back into heat twenty-one days after her failed mating. In either case, if you notice that she has come back into heat, return her to the stud buck.

Once your goat is pregnant, you'll want to take special care with her nutrition. She needs the proper ratio of calcium and phosphorus to ensure that she can create lovely new sets of teeth and bone for her new kids. Refer to Chapter 7 for details.

Rick Misterly of Quillisascut Farm holds a newborn kid as her mother conscientiously licks her clean.

CHAPTER NINE

THE KIDDING MIRACLE

KIDDING IS THE MOST EXCITING PART OF GOAT KEEPING. The suspense of it is terrible, but when all goes well, you will be rewarded with tiny new lives covered in goop, struggling to stand, and searching intently for their mother's teats with great persistence but little skill. Your new baby goats will be so cute and adorable that you will hardly be able to stand it. You will watch as their tiny tails wiggle with contentment as they finally find their mother's teat and taste their first sip of sustenance. You will see your goat, a tired but conscientious new mother, instinctively lick her babies until they are gorgeous and gleaming and fluffy. With the birth of new kids, your goat shed will be transformed into a domestic paradise sure to warm the heart of anyone lucky enough to enter.

While kidding is a joyous and exciting time, sometimes it can be too exciting, leaving those who should have their wits about them mushy and jittery and unable to think straight. For this reason, it is important to be prepared and know what to expect.

Be There

Although goats are generally able to give birth by themselves with no problem, sometimes things go wrong, and you should be there to help out. Even if you don't know how to "go in" and reposition kids, there is still much a novice can do to assist. Sometimes kids have mucus covering their nostrils that, for whatever reason, the mother doesn't notice and clear. If this happens, you'll be able to save a life simply by wiping a nose. Sometimes, especially after a difficult birth, your goat's mothering instinct may not kick in, and she'll leave her kids to starve to death. If you are around, you may be able to jump-start her mothering instincts, and if you can't do that, you can take care of the kids yourself by drying them off and bottle-feeding them colostrum. In short, there are very small things anyone can do to save the lives of newborn goats, so even if you feel helpless, you aren't and should do all you can to be at your goat's side for her birthing.

To help make sure you don't miss the birth, mark down the date of her breeding and calculate the due date. Goats generally give birth between 143 and 155 days after breeding. There are many online calculators that help you determine day 150 (see the Goaty Resources section at the end of this book for some of these), or you can just count off days using a calendar. The day of breeding is counted as day 1.

I once took my goat Maple to a stud buck, and all went well, but then she came into heat again twenty-one days later. Since it appeared she hadn't settled, I took her to the stud buck a second time, and again all appeared to go well. Because she had gone into heat and mated a second time, I assumed that the first mating had not taken, and I calculated her day of kidding from the date of the second mating. Strangely, it turned out that the first mating *had* actually taken. As her pregnancy progressed, I began to suspect that this might be the case, but I figured it was wishful thinking, and on what was day 146 from the first breeding, I took an afternoon excursion out of town to visit a friend. When I came home, there were two dead kids on the goat shed floor and one barely hanging on. I tried desperately to save the new kid by warming her up and tube-feeding her colostrum, but she died within two hours. The next day, Maple came down with a uterine infection. I still don't know what happened—did a stillborn kid cause the infection? How long before my return had Maple given birth? Did the kids die of cold? Could they not find the teat? Were the kids born dead? I am plagued by these questions. If I had been more experienced, I would have realized that Maple was indeed close to kidding, and I would have been there.

HOW TO KNOW WHEN KIDDING STARTS

On the other side of the coin, Snowflake has given birth three times, and every time I have missed the actual birth, though not for want of trying. This is not uncommon, because some does don't want to give birth unless they have privacy. Whether they do want privacy or don't seem to care, it's very helpful to have a baby monitor. With a baby monitor, you can listen to what's happening in the goat shed without actually being there, and your goat will be none the wiser. You don't need the kind with a camera; one with only sound will work perfectly well. Through the monitor you'll hear lots of pawing and shuffling around. Sometimes you'll hear a soft bleating that goat mothers use to "talk" to their kids, even while the kids are still in utero. These sounds mean that kidding will probably occur in anywhere from twenty minutes to a week. If you hear a loud yell or groaning, get down to the goat shed!

There are also other signs, aside from a very loud and distinctive groaning, that can be helpful in gauging when kidding will occur. None, however, indicate such immediacy.

◆ **Mushy ligaments.** Well before your doe is ready to kid, feel for ligaments the thickness of a pencil around the base of her tail. These will loosen and almost disappear 12 to 24 hours before kidding.

◆ **Tail arching.** Tail arching is a sign of contractions. If you see a contraction, birthing should take place within the next several hours. Stick around.

◆ **Pawing.** Pawing is what goats do to prepare a nest for birthing, although I've never seen them actually use their nests. Some goats will begin intensive pawing within days of kidding, while others will begin pawing a week before kidding.

◆ **Baby talk.** Goats have a special, quiet bleat that they use for their kids. This chatting with their babies can begin about twelve hours before giving birth, or not until moments before.

◆ **Goop coming out of the vagina.** A clear goop will sometimes drip from the vagina. This is generally a sign that kidding will occur within the next few hours.

◆ **Panting.** Goats will often breathe heavily when they are in labor, as if they are overheated. Heavy breathing indicates labor has begun.

◆ **Mood swings.** Unaffectionate goats will sometimes become very affectionate, and affectionate goats will sometimes become aloof. Then it can all reverse again. This moodiness can occur a full week before kidding.

◆ **Licking.** When goats go into labor, their "clean the baby" instinct kicks in and they won't be able to get enough of licking you. While the incessant licking is just her cleaning instinct kicking in, it's hard not to feel that it's your goat's way of saying, "I am so happy you are here with me to help me through this trying and emotional time."

Kidding Preparations

Your goat needs a clean goat shed within which to give birth. Most how-to goat books recommend that you prepare a kidding stall. To most goat book authors, this is a totally separate shed or large space within your existing goat shed. Although a kidding stall is wonderful to have, it isn't necessary. If you have just two goats, you can use your goat shed as the kidding stall. However, you *must* clean it, especially if you have been using the deep bedding system. You'll have to take a pitchfork or a shovel and remove all those months' worth of bedding materials and poop and pee. This ends up being very dusty work, so wear a dust mask to protect your lungs. Have your compost bins standing by, and add water as you fill them to make sure that the entire pile of compost is dampened. Adding moisture will significantly speed up the composting process.

Once your goat shed is empty, carefully sweep it out and add new bedding. If your goat hasn't kidded within a few days of your cleaning, you'll need to clean it again. Given how difficult it is to predict when your goat will give birth, you may end up having to clean out the shed several times before the kids show up, so don't put in too much new bedding, just enough to make your goat comfortable. You do not need to use bleach to sanitize your goat shed, but you want to sweep out every bit of dust and poop that you can find.

If you have been using wood shavings as your bedding material, you may want to switch to straight straw, because the wood shavings will stick to the goopy newborns and make it tough to get them clean. Alternatively, some people try to slip a clean towel under the kid as it slides out. The trouble with straw is that it is difficult to remove from the shed and composts more slowly than wood shavings.

It's a good idea to have on hand the following items before your goat kids:

✔ **Surgical scrub,** such as Betadine, to wash your hands.

✔ **7 percent iodine solution** (for cleaning and sterilizing the cut umbilical cord).

✔ **Dental floss** (to tie off the cut umbilical cord).

✔ **A sterilized film canister** or a similar shaped container to use for dipping the umbilical cord.

✔ **Sterilized scissors** (to cut the umbilical cord).

✔ **Clean, dry towels** (that you wouldn't mind getting stained) to help dry the kids off and to use as a landing pad when they drop out.

Goat births tend to go well, with mother and kids behaving as if they've memorized a textbook on the subject. However, sometimes things go wrong, so make sure to have on hand:

❷ **The contact information and directions for your goat vet** and an emergency goat vet who is available in the dead of night.

❷ **Colostrum or colostrum replacer.** Colostrum is the precursor to milk, and a doe gives it for only a few days after giving birth. It is yellowish in color and extremely rich, and helps boost the newborn kids' immune systems.

❷ **A human baby bottle** with the hole in the tip of the nipple cut slightly larger, or better yet a Pritchard nipple (available through goat supply catalogs) and bottle (see the "Bottle Feeding" section).

Many people also recommend having on hand a feeding tube with a 60 ml syringe for tube-feeding a weak kid. However, using one is very tricky, and if you use it incorrectly, you can easily kill the newborn kid by filling her lungs with milk. If you are a beginner, it's probably best to simply make sure you can get a kid to a vet within an hour or two should it be born weak. If you have some medical background and are brave, there is an excellent article on tube-feeding in *Goat Health Care* by Cheryl Smith (see the Goaty Resources section at the end of the book).

ENJOY THOSE KIDS!

Make sure the kids have lots of time with their mother and plenty of time to nap, but feel free to pick them up and hold them. Sometimes they'll fall asleep in your arms if you sit down. A friend of mine used to try to let the kids come to her first, but after raising several kids who never did come to her, she gave up and began just picking up the newborns. This worked great, and mother and kid didn't mind a bit. Mothers will often get nervous if you move too far away with the kid, so when you pick up a kid, don't take it beyond its mother's reach.

If your goat-keeping experience goes anything like mine, you will have friends ask if they can come watch the birth. Although it's tempting to say yes, it's best to refuse. Your goats may not like having even you around, let alone strangers or near strangers. It's best to promise these people that they can come over after the birth (but not all at once). Should a friend who also happens to be an obstetrician or a delivery nurse ask you to watch the birth, you may want to say yes. Even if these people don't have goat experience, they'll have knowledge that may help you.

When the Kids Arrive

Once the kids slide out and you wipe the tears from your eyes as you wonder what sort of life they will lead and what their future will hold, you will want to do what you can to make sure that everyone in the family has what they need. Here are a few things to attend to:

- **Make sure that there is no goo covering the kid's mouth or nostrils** and preventing it from breathing. (This is something you should attend to before wiping any tears from your own eyes.)

- **Offer the new mother a treat:** a clean bucket of warm water with a few tablespoons of molasses mixed in as an after-birth refreshment and treat.

- **Cut the umbilical cord:** If the kid has an umbilical cord that hangs more than an inch from its belly, or if the umbilical cord didn't break at all, use a pair of sterilized sharp scissors and cut it 1 inch from the belly. Use a piece of dental floss to tie it off at the end, and then dip the entire length of the cord in a 7 percent iodine solution.

◢ Find those teats! Stay with the mother and kids until each new kid has found a teat and gotten a nice long drink. If, after fifteen minutes, you notice any kids still poking around with their mouths to no effect, help guide them. While they will be quite persistent with their poking, they will miss and miss and miss. Have patience. You can't stick their mouths on the teats, but you can try to get them aiming in the right direction and at the right end of their mother.

◢ Make sure the kids get clean. If the mother wanders off and doesn't immediately begin to clean her kids, see if you can kick-start her mothering instincts. Sometimes it works to rub a bit of the baby's goo onto the mother's nose and then to put her kids in front of her. If the mother won't clean off the kids, you should do so. Dry them off as quickly as you can so that they don't get cold.

◢ Make sure the kids get nursed. If for some reason the mother won't let a kid or kids nurse, you may need to bottle-feed. However, before you resort to the bottle, try putting the mother in the milking stand and then help the kids up to nurse. This way, the

Newborn kids struggle to stand in the first few hours of their lives but within just a few days, they can gambol about the goat yard doing flips.

mother can't run off. If you still can't help the kids get milk from their mother, you'll need to milk out the mother and bottle-feed her milk (colostrum at this point) to the kids. The colostrum must be at goat body temperature (102 degrees F.) for the kids to take it.

❡ **Your goat should deliver her placenta within twelve hours after kidding.** Before it falls off, it will hang from her vagina for several hours or more. Do not be tempted to pull it out as this may cause tearing. Once it does come off, she will probably try to eat it. There are different schools of thoughts on this, but generally, it's a good idea to let her eat at least some of the placenta. If your goat does not deliver her placenta within twelve hours of kidding, bring her to a vet. She may have a stillborn inside her.

Once your new goat babies have exited their mother's womb and appear to be eating well and to have developed a positive relationship with their mother, you can exhale and take a few days' rest. You'll want to disbud the kids when they are three to four days old and neuter the males when they are eight weeks old, but otherwise, aside from needing to keep an eye on the new family's well-being, you can sit back and let the goat

The bond between mother goat and kid is a thing of beauty.

mother take care of everything. Assuming that you have only one or two other adult goats, you can let the kids and mother out into their herd within a few hours of the birth. Goat aunts are usually not particularly loving and are, as a general rule, exceedingly discipline oriented. Should a new kid make the mistake of bounding into its aunt, the aunt will toss all diplomatic solutions aside and give the kid a butt. This is simply the way of goats.

Bottle-Feeding

There are times when you will have no option but to bottle-feed. Sometimes the mother flat-out rejects a kid. If you have done all you can to get the mother goat to allow her kid to nurse, and the mother simply won't, you'll need to step in with a bottle.

If you don't have a commercial goat nipple, such as the Pritchard nipple, available, you can use a human baby bottle and modify the nipple by using a razor blade to very slightly increase the hole size. Ideally, have a Pritchard nipple on hand. These are made for ewes and screw onto standard disposable water bottles; they are available through goat supply catalogs.

For the first few days, your kid will need colostrum instead of milk. You can sometimes buy this in frozen form from experienced goat keepers. You can also buy

GUIDE TO BOTTLE-FEEDING A NEWBORN KID

AGE OF KID	WHAT TO FEED	INITIAL AMOUNT PER FEEDING	GRADUALLY WORK UP TO	FREQUENCY OF FEEDING
Days 1 and 2	Warm colostrum	½ cup	¾ cup	Every 4 hours around the clock
Days 3 and 4	Warm colostrum and milk combined	1 cup	1¼ cups	5 times per day between 7:00 AM and 9:00 PM
Weeks 1 and 2	Warm milk	1½ cups	1¾ cups	3 times per day between 7:00 AM and 7:00 PM
Weeks 2 through 6	Milk	2 cups	2½ cups	2 times per day between 7:00 AM and 7:00 PM
Weeks 6 through 8	Milk	2½ cups	0 (weaning)	2 times per day between 7:00 AM and 7:00 PM

Source: Jack Mauldin, an experienced goat keeper in Texas, who operates the website www.jackmauldin.com.

colostrum replacer, but it doesn't have the antibodies of real colostrum. If at all possible, milk colostrum from the kid's mother and use that. Whatever you do, make sure it is warm, 102 degrees F. If you milk it from the mother, and you know or worry that the mother might be ill, pasteurize the colostrum by heating it to 160 degrees F for 30 seconds. Then bring it down to 102 degrees as quickly as possible. Whatever you do, *do not* microwave it. Microwaving can create hot spots in the milk, and some argue that it destroys nutrients and antibodies.

To give a kid a bottle, position the kid and the bottle in such a way that it needs to raise its head to drink. It should be in the same position it would be in if it was nursing from its mother—that is, reaching up a bit. Sit cross-legged and hold the kid in your lap, with its bottom down and front legs up. Place one hand just under the kid's chin, raising it up slightly. With the other hand, hold the bottle. Insert the nipple into the kid's mouth. *Do not* pour the milk in, or squirt it out in a stream. It's okay to squirt just a single drop to give the kid an inkling of what the bottle contains. However, be careful. If you squirt too much, it can flow into the kid's lungs. Sometimes getting a goat to take

Sometimes, for reasons unknown, a mother will reject her kids and you will have to bottle-feed.

IT'S OKAY TO PAY A VET OR EXPERIENCED FARMER

In reading goat books written by goat keepers with decades of experience and tens to hundreds of goats, I found so much advice on tricky maneuvers that I began to think that all real goat owners should be able to reach deep into a goat's birth canal to untangle kids, disbud kids using a high-temperature skull scalder, and then, to top off their afternoon, slice open a young buckling's genitals to remove his testicles. In retrospect, while these skills are very good to know, I've come to the conclusion that you can be a real and respectable goat owner and pay someone to do these things for you. If you have just a few goats, and especially if you have only one set of kids born each year, taking them in for disbudding and neutering is often simpler and less expensive than buying the equipment necessary and tackling these jobs yourself. If you feel determined to learn these skills, feel free to do so. But for the sake of your goats, make sure you know enough to do a very good job. Lastly, before picking up any scalders or scalpels, it's best to find someone who knows what they are doing, and watch and listen and learn. (See Chapter 12.)

a bottle is extremely difficult, but it is less difficult with kids who have never latched onto a real nipple. Be patient and keep trying.

Once your kid gets its first taste of milk, it should become enthusiastic about milking sessions. When it turns two weeks old, it may begin to accept cold milk as opposed to warm.

Preparing the Goat Yard for Kids

A mother goat will take care of almost all of her kids' needs, but you may need to make a few changes to your goat yard when the kids arrive. Kids can easily climb through a stock panel fence with 5-by-8-inch partitions. They can even make it through combo panels aimed specifically at preventing their escape. Unless you have stock panel with 4-by-4-inch partitions, you'll need to line the bottom 2 feet of your fence with welded wire or chicken wire. To feel safe from the less friendly adults in their herd, goat kids enjoy small enclosed spaces in which to nap together. A dog crate or old coffee table can provide a comforting den-like atmosphere.

At as young as three days old, goat kids begin tasting hay and browse, and within a week or two they may try drinking water. So put a small stash of hay, alfalfa pellets, and water at kid level. Mother goat will take care of all the rest.

Stealing Milk from the Kids

After about five days (three days if there is just one kid), if the kids look strong and healthy, you'll want to begin separating them from their mother at night. You can use an extra-large dog crate that you put in the goat shed, or you can partition off a section of the goat shed for the kids. A partitioned area of the goat shed works best because it allows room for you to provide water and hay. The idea is to prevent the kids from nursing from their mothers while keeping mother and kids within nose-touching distance of one another. Although this may feel a bit harsh, in my experience, the kids and mother settle right down, and the mother even seems to appreciate her break.

For the first night, lock the kids away from their mother for only eight hours, and just before you let them out, milk out the mother. (See Chapter 11 for complete milking instructions.) Don't be tempted to leave any milk for the kids. If you do this, they'll anxiously await being let out each day, and this could cause them, and subsequently their mother, to make lots of noise every morning, starting at sunup. Also, if they learn that their mother's teats are chock-full in the morning, they'll fight hard for a teat and even hang onto it with their teeth. This will, as you might expect, displease their

Kids enjoy small denlike areas, like this hen's nesting box, where their aunts won't step on them and they can stay warm.

mother. Only after the mother is carefully milked out should you release the kids. They will immediately go to their mother and nurse. They won't get much, but as the day goes on, they'll get plenty.

The second night, keep the kids separated from their mother for ten hours, and on the third night, keep them separated for twelve hours. My goat mentor Laura Workman of Glimmercroft Farm has been fine-tuning this dam-raising method for fifteen years. She notes that it is extremely important in terms of udder and teat development for the mother and kids to be separated for a full twelve hours. During the first two months of a goat's lactation, her udder and teats can be stretched and will grow if milk is allowed to build up inside. By allowing twelve hours' worth of milk production to build up, you are helping stretch the udder and teats. In addition, by taking twelve hours' worth of milk every day from the doe, you are putting extra demand on her production, and her body will crank up to meet those demands. The dairy goat has been domesticated for thousands of years, so don't feel that you are asking too much of her. It is part of her heritage to produce milk for her kids *and* her caretaker. If you simply let the kids nurse twenty-four hours a day for eight weeks before sending them away, and then you begin the milking routine, you will get much less milk for yourself. More importantly, your doe's udder and teats will not grow to their potential, meaning that what little milk you do get for her entire lactation will be far more difficult to milk out.

Workman theorizes that the goat's body may release a hormone during the first two months of lactation that allows for the stretching of the teats and udder. This would explain the relatively small window of opportunity for udder and teat development. She's also found that after the first two freshenings, it's not possible to expand the teat and udder further. Note: A freshening is when the goat has kidded and begun to give milk anew. The milk supply is refreshed; hence, the word *freshening*.

Weaning

I have often read that goat mothers naturally wean their kids, and that you should not interfere with this beautiful and natural process. While this may work for some people, the two people I know who have tried it now have doelings that are still nursing well into their second year. Although I believe there are goats out there who take care of the weaning issue themselves, my experience strongly suggests that you cannot count on having such a goat. In addition, it is much easier to foil the nursing attempts of a 15-pound kid than a 100-pound goat.

If you are selling your kids and they leave by the time they are eight to ten weeks old, you don't have to worry about weaning them. The problem will take care of itself

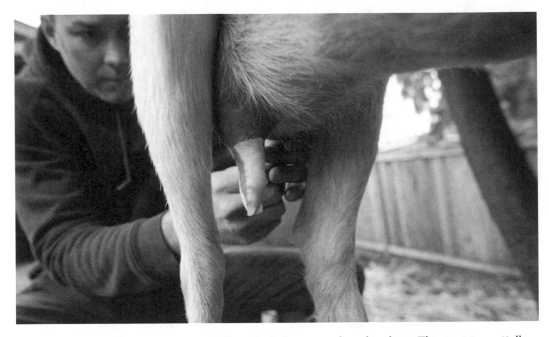

Tom Clauson applies teat tape to Molly to help her wean her daughter. This teat is partially taped. Tom will attach a second piece of tape loosely around the circumference of the teat.

when the kids move away. However, if you decide to keep a kid or the new owners are not able to bring the kids to their new home for several months, you'll want to assist the mother with the weaning process. You don't need to worry about introducing solid food to kids. If hay or foliage is within their reach, they'll begin to eat it when they are ready (usually when they are only a few days old).

You can physically separate mother and kids for a week by adding a stock panel division to your goat yard, but this can be tricky if there's any rain, because they'll both need access to the goat shed. Also, it separates them, which both mother and kids will dislike. My favorite solution to the weaning problem is teat tape.

You can buy teat tape from goat supply catalogs, but you can also buy the paper surgical tape sold at pharmacies. Just make sure not to buy plastic surgical tape. If a kid somehow ingested plastic tape, it could become wedged in one of the openings between the goat's stomachs and cause serious problems.

Messing with teat tape twice a day may sound like a royal pain, but once you have tried it a few times you will find it relatively simple to use. After milking, you clean and dry the teat and then apply a strip of teat tape vertically so it covers the hole. After that, you add a strip horizontally, around the teat. When applying the horizontal piece, stretch the teat gently while applying it so that you don't wrap it too tight. Remember, the teat is going to fill and stretch, and you don't want to strangle it.

You can fold the ends of the vertical strips of teat tape over by an eighth of an inch at each end to create tabs for easy removal. However, it's best not to create such tabs for the first few days you use the tape, since the kids are going to be working very hard to get that tape off, and they might grab hold of the tiny tabs. After a few days of trying their best without any luck in getting the tape off, the kids' persistence will dwindle and they'll stop working so hard to nurse. This is when you can start using the tabs. After a few more weeks, you can probably get by with just using the vertical tape. How long you will need to use teat tape depends on your kids. Some people need to use it for only a week, while others have to use it for as long as the mother goat is in milk. You'll need to experiment to find out where your kids fit on the teat tape spectrum.

Finding Homes for the Kids

When it's time to sell your kids, you may get lucky and find a home for them through word of mouth. However, you will probably need to advertise. I've always used Craigslist—it's really the best way to advertise and is where everyone now goes in the urban (and rural) small farming trade. Be sure to include cute pictures and to discuss the mother goat's dairy abilities (unless the kid is a wether) and the kid's affectionate and inquisitive nature. Always charge for the goats to help ensure that whoever buys them is serious about wanting them. You can also post a notice at your local feed store—most keep bulletin boards for customers to advertise their livestock. If your city has a Yahoo! group of gardening or chicken buffs, you can get the word out that way with a short email. Try your best to screen the potential home:

⦿ How much research have the prospective buyers done?

⦿ Do they have realistic expectations?

⦿ Do they own their home? If not, how long have they been in their rental, and what does their landlord think of having goats on the property?

⦿ What other animals do they have? How long have they had them, and what sort of care do their animals get?

⦿ If someone wants to buy your goat to eat it, how do they propose to kill it?

❷ **If you are selling it to someone who has a goat land-clearing business,** find out how long they keep their goats working and what they do with the goats when they reach retirement age.

In the end, even the most carefully vetted potential owners may find that goat keeping is not for them. This is inevitable, but do your best to find someone who will do all they can to make sure your goats lead a healthy, happy life or, if they plan to butcher the goats, that they know what they are doing.

I'm often asked what will happen when the market for dairy goats becomes saturated. If the number of available kids begins to outpace the number of available homes, this may become a problem. However, given that people do eat goats, and given that humanely raising and dispatching goats is preferable to tossing factory-farmed meat into your grocery cart, goat overpopulation shouldn't become a serious issue.

If you decide to butcher and eat your young goats, you will need to do some research on how to kill them humanely. Because goats have very thick skulls, shooting them in the head requires a certain level of knowledge about guns and skill in using them. The same is true for slitting a goat's throat. Some areas have rules about discharging firearms, so check with your police department before you take this route. You may need to take your goat out to the country if you plan to shoot it. As for butchering, you can hire a butcher to dispatch a goat for you, but if you do so, have them come to you. Moving is very stressful to goats, especially if they are penned up with other animals they don't know. Experienced hunters often know how to prepare a carcass for eating, and you might be able to find a hunter who can help you.

Whatever you do, do not sell your goat at auction. The pens at farm auction houses are not nice places.

Eloise was able to stay with her mother at the Goat Justice League Farm; she looks forward to a career as a dairy goat.

Melissa Clauson milks a beautifully trained Molly. Some people milk from behind while others choose to milk from the side.

CHAPTER TEN

THE TAMING OF THE GOAT

ALTHOUGH LOTS OF DAIRY GOAT OWNERS-TO-BE research the hand motion of milking (covered in Chapter 11), few look into how to get their goat to hold still while they milk. I know lots of people who have gone about their goat keeping in a very organized way. They read books, visit people with goats, carefully build sheds and fences, select lovely and sensible goats, breed them with fine studs, and birth the babies. And then, when it comes time to actually milk the goat, they realize that they have no idea how to get their goat onto the milking stand, much less how to get milk out of the goat. After managing to wrestle the goat onto the stand, they inevitably are surprised to find that their goat kicks like a wild bronco whenever they reach to touch her udder.

Why would a dairy goat behave in such a decidedly undairy-goat-like manner? It is because dairy goats, being reasonable creatures, want to give milk only to their own children, and they know enough to know that you are not their kid. As a result, you must teach your goat something that goes against their nature, and this can be difficult and frustrating at times.

You need to be prepared to train your goat to behave on the milking stand. If you don't, your goat will train you. To drive this concept home, I'll tell you about my cousin Jim Christie. Jim is not your typical goat owner. Most of the goat owners I know are women and are interested in things like organic food, and Jim is neither. He is a naval nuclear submarine captain who lives in a small town outside Bremerton, Washington. He is six foot four, 185 pounds of pure muscle, and can rip a Seattle telephone book in half. He also runs marathons and does century bike rides. But when he's not being super-tough, commanding people, and generally defending the free world, he can often be found out in his goat yard, tending to his very small herd of dairy goats.

Jim purchased his herd, a pair of doelings, from me after he discovered that cow milk didn't agree with his stomach but that goat milk did. He didn't like the taste of storebought goat milk, but he loved super-fresh goat milk. Hence, when my Brownie gave birth to a pair of fine doelings, he stepped right up, purchased the pair, and named them Agatha and Daphne. Although he has a commanding presence that leads every sailor under his command to "hop to" when he enters a room, Jim had a problem when it came to commanding Daphne and Agatha. I learned about his "goat command" issues when I milked his goats one weekend while he and I did a house exchange. We'd come up with the idea to save money on our vacations. The idea was that he and his family would stay at my house to enjoy the city, and my family and I would stay at his house to enjoy the country. Since we were exchanging houses, we also exchanged goat-milking duties. He milked Snowflake, and I milked Daphne. (Agatha was not in milk at the time.)

Sadly, the exchange did not go smoothly on my end. The first morning that I tried to milk Daphne, she rebelled. Daphne, who I had helped bring into the world and who was an otherwise sweet and docile goat, turned into a wild beast on the milking stand. She kicked the pail of milk over several times, sat down in the pail, and generally thrashed about every time I laid a hand on her teats. I don't know how I ever did get her milked out, but an hour after I'd gone humming into that goat shed, I stumbled out with only a cup of milk in my bottle and several cups on my clothing. I had decided not to tell Jim how horrible Daphne was, because I didn't want to be rude. And when he and his family returned, I managed to hold my tongue for a full ten minutes. Then, throwing caution to the wind, I said something like, "Daphne is horrible on the milking stand." Jim, who despite being a tough and macho naval officer was blindingly in love with Daphne, responded with something like, "Yes, isn't she wonderful?" so I left it at that.

The next spot of trouble happened when I was at a dinner party at Jim's house and his sister, my cousin Ruth Anne, was there too. Ruth Anne wanted to learn to milk, so Jim offered to let her practice on Daphne. This was obviously not a good idea, so I butted into their conversation and said, "Ruth Anne, don't practice on Daphne. She's horrible on the milking stand."

Jim gave me a withering look and said, "Daphne just has some preferences. She likes to be milked one-handed."

Despite Jim's phone book tearing abilities, I said, "That's not a preference. That's not trained. I can't believe that you, a guy with nuclear capabilities, are letting a mini-dairy goat set her own milking rules."

Jim ignored me and turned to Ruth Anne and said, "Daphne also likes you to dribble in her food very slowly, and it helps her relax if you do yoga chants."

Tricks of the Trade

Now, to be entirely honest, my two goats at the time, Brownie and Snowflake, were not perfect on the milking stand. I would give them a few cups of their concentrate to eat while they were being milked, and they would be very cooperative—until their concentrate ran out. I was able to work around this by adding hydrated beet pulp to their concentrate. (Hydrated beet pulp is simply beet pulp pellets that have been soaked in water. Beet pellets are made from sugar beet fibers, which are remnants of the sugar manufacturing process. They are high in fiber but low in calories, so they work well to keep goats busy on the milking stand.) Because I could milk Snowflake and Brownie out quickly while they ate their enhanced concentrate, I never had a problem. In this sense, Snowflake and Brownie trained me to be a very fast milker.

Several months after I first milked Daphne, Jim and I traded houses and milking duties again. This time I tried the beet pulp trick on Daphne, but she turned her nose up at it. Next, I tried giving her her concentrate all at once instead of dribbling it in. She looked at the concentrate and then looked at me and stomped with impatience. So I decided to try to go along with her "preferences." Alas, she must have known that I lacked respect for her "preferences," because even with Jim's one-handed, dribble-feeding, yoga-chanting method, things did not go well. In fact, they went so badly that I was left with no choice but to do something dramatic. In a stroke of good luck, I had recently heard an interesting milk-stand manners training tip from my farrier, Rebecca Hazzard, via my goat mentor, Laura. It was this—if the goat kicked, you grabbed her rear legs and gently lifted them a few inches up off the milking stand. This wouldn't hurt the goat but would make her uncomfortable.

I decided to try this method on Daphne. I put her head into the stanchion, poured 2 cups of concentrate into her dish, and knelt down to milk two-handed. She balked and kicked, so I set the milking pail aside, took hold of her two back legs, and lifted them up. She did not like this one bit and *really* thrashed around, but I held fast until she settled. Then I set her hooves back down and tried milking again. Again she recoiled, so again I lifted up her back legs. We went through this leg-lifting/struggling/milking/kicking cycle again and again. It was probably after the fifth such round that she allowed me to milk her two-handed for a minute or two. As we continued this pattern over the weekend, the time she spent struggling shortened, and the time she'd allow me to milk without fussing lengthened. I could tell the method was working, and it was working much faster than I could have hoped. By the time Jim returned (just four milking sessions later), Daphne required only five leg lifts per milking. She was a new goat.

I was ecstatic about conquering Daphne's strong-willed ways, and Daphne seemed glad too. Now she stood patiently and seemed far less anxious. I could not wait to show Jim, but could I tell Jim that his goats were undisciplined and insist that he use my new method?

Given that I would have to milk Daphne in the future if I wanted to continue our home exchanges, which I did want to do, I decided that I would need to be straightforward. So I wrote what I thought was a tactful but to-the-point note for Jim and left it on his counter. It said, "Daphne was a monster on the milking stand. She's on a new training regime. Call me in the morning, before you milk, and I'll explain to you the new milking procedure."

Jim must have been pretty frustrated with Daphne and her "preferences" himself, because his response to the note was, "So how do we do this?"

Once your goat has developed reliably good milking stand manners, you can cut a hole in the floor of your milking stand and milk directly into a bottle (filter on top).

I talked Jim through the leg-lift trick, and at first he did not like it at all and kept telling me that the only good part about it was that he was getting an amazing workout for his biceps (which was true; Daphne could give you a great biceps workout). He told me that if things kept going as they were, he'd be able to rip a New York City phone book in half. But he kept with it, implementing what he called a zero-tolerance policy, and quite quickly, Daphne got the message. At long last, she settled into her role as a dairy goat, and from that point forward, I am proud to say, she has behaved like an angel on the milking stand.

So if you want a Zenlike bonding-with-a-goat milking experience, know that you may have to go through some very non-Zenlike times first. Know that you may need to wrestle about with your goat, hanging madly onto her hooves with the determination of a cowboy riding a bucking bronco at a rodeo. When things with your goat get tough like this, just remember, like many of life's struggles, it's worth it.

How to Train Your Goat Before Your Goat Trains You

About two months before your goat gives birth, you will want to begin giving her just a cup of concentrate twice a day—one in the morning and one in the evening. As noted in Chapter 7, concentrate is a commercial goat chow, such as Purina Mills Goat Chow or Nutrena Top Goat. Goats love their concentrate. A concentrate to a goat is like ice cream to a human—it is far richer in calories than the leaves and grass that constitute the bulk of their diet.

GET YOUR GOAT COMFORTABLE ON THE MILKING STAND

To get your goat to hop onto the stand and put her head through the stanchion, place her daily 1 cup of concentrate in the cup that's mounted on the milking stand. Your goat may try to get at the ration without getting onto the stand itself, so you may need to gently block her in various ways until she finally hops up and slips her head through the stanchion to nibble away. As soon as she does this, lock your stanchion closed so she can't get her head out. This might bother her a little, but with the concentrate in a bowl just under her nose, she will settle down and simply eat. As soon as she's through eating, unlock the stanchion and release her.

Some goats may not want to get onto the stand, no matter what. If this is the case, find someone to help you lift her up. Lock her in the stanchion, let her eat, and while she's eating, give her a nice scratch or brush her if she enjoys being brushed. After a day or two of this, she should become more enthusiastic about the experience. The idea here is to help her associate being on the milking stand with the good life.

PRACTICE TOUCHING YOUR GOAT'S TEATS

After a week or two of getting your goat accustomed to hopping onto the milking stand to enjoy her daily ration of concentrate, you can begin the next step.

Once she's up, locked in, and chowing down, give her a nice scratch and then try touching her udder with your two hands. She may not like this—at all—but just put your hands there and keep them there until she decides it's not so bad. If possible, try to make sure your hands aren't cold. After a few days (or weeks) of this, after touching her udder, place your hands gently on her teats. With time she will learn that this isn't so bad either. It's a good idea to get her used to your touching her teats a good month before she actually gives birth. During the few weeks just before kidding, she may develop sensitive teats, and so you'll want to acclimate her to having her teats touched well before this. With luck, your goat will come to think that you are a strange but harmless creature.

Rebellious Dairy Goats

Even if you've managed to get your goat accustomed to having her teats and udder touched, she may still give you a hard time when it comes to milking. There are goats who simply seem to know they were born to be dairy goats. They will hop onto their milking platform and stand peaceably as you milk, contented with their lot in life. However, such goats are the exception. If your goat is not one of these exceptions and balks at her dairy destiny, you'll want to know about four different techniques for working with a rebellious dairy goat at milking time: hydrated beet pulp, treats only for good behavior, restraints, and leg lifts.

HYDRATED BEET PULP AS FILLER

Hydrated beet pellets are a harmless but tasty filler. They are made from the remnants of beet sugar manufacturing. By mixing your goat's concentrate with hydrated beet pellets, you can slow her eating and thereby buy yourself more time to milk her out. To do this, take ½ cup of beet pellets, put them in a 4-cup container, add 1 cup of water, and let the mixture sit for a few hours or overnight. You will be impressed by how much the mixture expands. It

Beet pellets quadruple in volume when soaked for several hours. Both these measuring cups contain a quarter cup of beet pulp, but the one in the rear has expanded to the one-cup mark due to the addition of a quarter cup of water.

will have a lot of volume, but not too many calories and lots of good fiber. You then mix the hydrated beet pulp with the concentrate. This method usually works beautifully, with the average goat so enthusiastic about it that she stands quietly, chowing down while you milk. However, some goats don't like the beet pulp and get so miffed about their concentrate being watered down in this way that they will do some serious fussing until you give them their usual non-watered-down fare or embark on actual training.

THE CARROT APPROACH

I found this method very difficult to implement, but it did work for a friend of mine: Give your goat her concentrate only *after* you are finished milking. Goat owners who've had success with this approach teach their goats that to get their concentrate, they must stand still and get milked out. The idea is that once your goat has been still for a short time and allows you to milk, you give her a "carrot," or treat, in the form of some concentrate. Then you milk some more, rewarding her with more concentrate if she behaves. Slowly, you work the rewards farther and farther apart until you are giving the reward only after you are finished milking. This method requires two people—one to dispense the concentrate and one to do the milking.

RESTRAINTS

Some goats aren't going to accept their concentrate being watered down with beet pulp and will get too ramped up by the carrot system to even think of behaving well. If your goat is like this, you should begin by trying one of two restraint systems.

The best-known restraint system uses a hobble. A hobble is a device that connects the legs of a goat together, making it more difficult for her to kick. A primitive hobble can be made with a piece of twine, but twine can too easily dig into the skin of a goat and so is not recommended. More advanced hobbles are made with wide nylon webbing and Velcro. Hobbles work on some goats, but I've found them frustrating to use. Although they connect the goat's two back legs together, they can agitate a goat into kicking wildly—albeit, with both legs together.

Less well known than hobbles are cable clamps. These are made for bundling together electrical and computer cables rather than for training goats, but they can be easily retrofitted into excellent goat restraints. You can find them at most hardware stores or online. They are plastic rings that click open and closed and that can be ratcheted to fit perfectly around a goat's hoof. Laura Workman came up with a very simple, clever, and inexpensive solution using cable clamps and twine that can quiet even the most rebellious goats. I fit the cable clamps onto the goat's hooves and then lace the cable clamp with clothesline through an eyehook and fasten it with a cleat (the type found on sailboats) that is screwed to the milking stand.

Generally, the need for a restraint system is temporary. Once your goat gets used to you milking her and learns that it relieves the discomfort of her full udder, she will stop struggling and you can set the restraint system aside.

LEG LIFTS

As a last resort, you can try the leg-lift system that I used to train the irascible Daphne. This system works like a charm but is not for the faint of heart. It requires strong arms and determination.

To use this system, begin milking your goat. As soon as she begins to kick, and she may begin the moment you touch her teat, whisk your pail out of the way, and with each hand grab a back leg and lift them a few inches off the stand, so that she's doing

If your goat kicks while you are milking, set aside the milk pail and lift her rear hooves off the milking stand. She won't like it and will learn to stand still during milking if you are consistent.

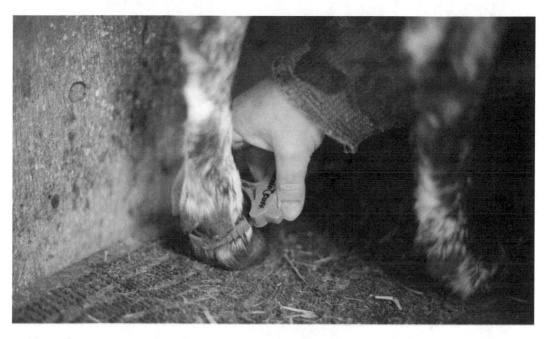

Cable cuffs are meant to bundle cables, but they also work well to hold hooves down on poorly behaved goats. Attach a cord to the cuff, cuff the goat between her dew claw and hoof, and then tie the cord down to the milking stand.

a sort of handstand or wheelbarrow. She will not like this *at all* and may kick about even more. Here's where you hold on and it becomes you against the goat. Hang on to her back legs until she stops struggling and settles. As soon as she does, put her down and try milking again. You'll need to continue this until you get her completely milked out. I was able to tell within a single milking session that this system would work with Daphne. I must have lifted her legs thirty times. By the next day, my biceps were very sore, but I was buoyed by the fact that she had seemed to develop a glimmer of understanding regarding what was expected of her. It often happens that in struggling to get milk from a goat, the struggle becomes personal. That's okay. Let it be personal. Just make sure that you are considerate and that you win in the end.

Understanding
how to milk is easy.
Becoming skilled
requires practice.

HOW TO MILK

MILKING REQUIRES MORE THAN A COOPERATIVE GOAT. It also requires equipment. To milk your goat, you'll need a milking stand (to contain the goat) and a milking stool (to sit on) as well as other milking paraphernalia. And you'll need to decide where to do the milking. If you have a small, one-room goat shed, and you use the deep bedding system, there's bound to be fecal matter dust in the air. Therefore, for sanitation reasons, it's best to have your milking stand outside the goat shed, in open air, but with a roof to keep the rain off you and your goat. Sometimes space limitations will mean that you have to milk in the goat shed. I did this for years without incident. However, open-air milking is preferable.

The Milking Stand

A milking stand is helpful in two ways:

🐐 It raises the goat to a level that makes it convenient for you to do the milking.

🐐 It holds the goat in place so she doesn't wander off while you are milking.

All milking stands need to be raised about 1½ feet off the ground and should be of solid and stable construction, be covered, and feature a locking stanchion to secure the goat's head during milking. I like to feed my goats their concentrate while they are being milked, so I also have a feeding dish attached to the stanchion. That way, while they are locked in, they are distracted with a snack.

You can buy a milking stand from a goat supply catalog (see Goaty Resources at the end of this book). These stands are made of metal and fold up, making them portable,

137

The milking stand

but they are more expensive than wooden milking stands. To find a wooden milking stand, you'll need to use Craigslist, where, in the Seattle area at least, there are a few people who advertise their homemade wooden stands. You can also often find used milking stands. If you are handy, you can even build one yourself. There are numerous instructions on the web for building them. See the Goaty Resources section. You can simplify milking stand construction by buying an inexpensive used coffee table, beefing it up with some supports, and then adding a stanchion made out of 1-by-2s.

THE MILKING KIT

A milking kit simply consists of the items used to milk your goat: some goat concentrate (such as Purina Mills Goat Chow), two rags or paper towels and soapy water, a strip cup, a milking pail with a top filter, and a wide-mouthed milk bottle or jar. I have all these items in my garage, which I head through on my way out to the goat yard, but many people keep their kit in the kitchen. Use a plastic dish tub to hold everything for carrying to the goat yard.

Milking pail. A pot with a steamer basket that sits inside works beautifully as a milking pail. The steamer nests perfectly inside the pot and is meant for vegetables. It looks like a double boiler but has holes for steam to travel through. The steamer inset keeps out bits of dirt and loose goat hair, prevents the milk from foaming, and if your goat acts up, can keep a hoof from ending up in the pail. It's important that the pail and steamer you use have no internal seams (seams on the outside for the handle are okay). The reason for this is sanitation. Tiny cracks from seams are impossible to clean properly. Some people purchase special milking pails with lids that have a small section cut out of the edge. These work well but are far more expensive than all-purpose pails, and are much more difficult to find secondhand. These dedicated milking pails are available through the major goat supply catalogs.

The milking kit shown here contains a half gallon mason jar, strainer with filter, concentrate, pot with steamer basket, teat disinfectant, diluted castile soap, and two clean rags. If your goat has dry skin on her teats, you'll want to include some udder balm too.

- **Milk bottle or jar.** I use a wide-mouthed, half-gallon mason jar for the milk. Any glass, enamel, or metal container with a wide mouth will work. Just make sure it doesn't have any seams and that it does have a tight-fitting lid.

- **Strainer with filter.** You want a strainer and filter made especially for milk. The filters are round disks made of an interwoven fabriclike mesh that traps debris while allowing milk to quickly pass through. They are thicker than paper coffee filters. The strainer holds the filter and sits neatly on top of the wide-mouthed mason jar. It is important to filter your goats' milk when you empty it from your pail into your jar, because even if you are practicing good sanitation and you've carefully cleaned your goat's udder, you will find that bits of hair and dirt will find their way from your goat into the filter. For sources, see the Goaty Resources section at the end of the book.

- **Two soft cloth towels.** Use chamois or a similar soft cloth, wetted with warm, soapy water, for cleaning the udder and teats. You can use paper towels, but if you do so, you'll need to use a good-quality brand that absorbs well and doesn't tear too easily. Pump a squirt or two of a foaming soap dispenser containing a mixture that is 1 part castile soap and 4 parts water onto your cloth. Then wet the whole rag and wring it out. You'll need two of these cloths, one for cleaning the udder and teats before milking and one for cleaning them after milking.

- **Udder balm.** Kids can be rough on their mother's teats and their constant suckling can dry out her skin. Added to this problem, her udder swells every night as it fills with milk and then shrinks down every morning when you milk her out. If her skin is dry, this expansion and contraction can lead to cracking. You can help alleviate this problem by applying udder balm or a thick hand cream (the type from a jar, not a squirt bottle) to her udder and teats every morning after milking and every evening, just after putting the kids to bed.

Milk strainer with filter

⊘ Teat disinfectant spray. I use Fight Bac disinfectant, but several brands are available from goat supply catalogs and some feed stores. Some people concoct their own teat dip by mixing a solution of mild soap and warm water. They pour the soapy water into a film canister and then dip the teat into the solution. This works well, but unlike a commercial teat spray like Fight Bac, it doesn't dry quickly.

⊘ Strip cup. A strip cup is any container into which you can squeeze the first few squirts of milk. It should be clear or white. The milk from the strip cup does not go into your milk bottle. Many people just throw it away. You can also feed it to your chickens. The reasons for the strip cup are twofold. First, the milk in the first few squirts has a much higher bacteria count than the rest of the flow, and for this reason it is best not to consume it. Second, you want to check the first few squirts to make sure that the milk isn't bloody, stringy, or bad smelling. These are all signs of mastitis, an infection of the mammary gland.

Once you get good at milking and your goat has developed good milking-stand manners, you can dispense with the milk pail and milk directly into the filter sitting atop your milk jar. To do this, you need to cut a circular hole into the milking stand so that you can set the jar lower than the surface that your goat is standing on. You'll also need something underneath the milking stand to hold the jar up so that it won't be too low. This system is nice in that it leaves you with two fewer items to wash.

Teaching Yourself to Milk

Milking takes much more practice than you would think. When people visit me and my goats, they often want to try their hand at milking. They watch me and think it looks easy, and then, when they try their hand at it, they discover that it's a struggle to extract even a quarter of a cup. This can be extremely discouraging, and almost everyone says something like, "I'm just no good at this."

As adults, we forget how difficult it is to learn a new skill involving coordination. Just like learning to ride a bike, type, or write in cursive, milking takes practice. Milking is not complicated, but it does take time to become fast, fluid, and effective. There's very little about milking that needs studying, but you will likely need to milk a goat a full ten times before you begin to feel confident. Also, many people master milking with one hand before the other and then just use that hand. Don't let this happen. If one hand becomes dominant, force yourself to milk with the other hand until it becomes masterful too.

When you begin milking, most likely your goat kids will be taking care of the day-time milking and you'll just be milking in the morning, after the kids have been separated from their mother overnight. Once the kids leave or are weaned at eight weeks old, you'll need to milk morning and night. It's best to milk every twelve hours, for example, at 7:00 AM and 7:00 PM, or at 8:00 AM and 8:00 PM. However, you don't need to be precise. Even if you regularly milk at 8:00 AM and 6:00 PM, it's not a problem to milk as late as 10:00 PM some nights if you've been out. However, as a general rule, for the sake of milk production and your doe's comfort, it's best not to let a goat go for more than 14 hours without being milked. This is especially true when she is producing at the peak of her lactation curve.

Once your goat is a few months past the peak of her lactation curve, usually about three months post-kidding, you can begin milking just once a day. You will get only one-half to two-thirds as much milk as you would get by milking twice a day. However, if you don't need all the milk your goats produce, and would enjoy some freedom from milking, once a day is a nice option.

SHAVING THE UDDER

Before you milk your goat for the first time (ideally a week or two before kidding), you'll want to shave around her udder. The idea is to keep hair out of the way when you're milking, to prevent you from pulling your goat's hair, and to cut down on dirt, which can attach to the hair and then fall into your milking pail. To trim, use hair-cutting clippers. You can buy these for around $25 at drugstores. Feed stores carry cordless clippers. These are nice to have but far more expensive than the ones with cords.

THE HAND MOTION

The idea behind milking is to trap the milk within the teat by pinching the top of the teat closed with your forefinger and thumb and then squeezing the milk out the small orifice at the bottom of the teat using your middle, ring, and pinky fingers. If you simply squeeze a teat without pinching it closed at the top, the milk will just flow back into the udder, and none will squirt out into your pail. Despite how milking is portrayed in the movies, there is no up-and-down motion involved. It's just pinch and squeeze. If you have a friend with a patient goat, it is a good idea to practice milking that goat before you need to milk your own.

Some people suggest using a pair of latex gloves to practice milking. With a pin, poke a hole in the end of a glove finger, fill the glove with water, and practice squeezing water out through the tiny new hole. It's not a great substitute for the real thing, but it will give you a sense of the importance of pinching off the top of the teat to

Your thumb and forefinger pinch the top of the teat closed, and your other fingers squeeze the milk out.

prevent the milk from going back up into the udder instead of into your milking pail.

When milking, make sure not to squeeze the flesh above the teat (the udder). The udder consists of mammary glands that are sensitive, and you can cause mastitis (an infection of the mammary gland) if you are too rough with the udder itself.

Milking a goat who is a first-time mother poses special difficulties. Their teats are very small at first, leaving little room for your pinky, ring, and index fingers. The teats are so small that you must milk with just your thumb, index, and middle finger. After several weeks, there should be more room for you to add your ring finger; after a few more months, you should be able to milk using your whole hand. Once your goat's teats reach their full size, more milk can be stored within them, and thus more milk can be squirted out per squeeze. When milking, you can squeeze each teat individually, alternating between the two: left teat, right teat; left teat, right teat. Alternatively, you can squirt both teats at the same time.

There's not too much more that can be said about the mechanics of milking. But know that your first few attempts are bound to be difficult and frustrating. Don't despair! You must keep at it, and when your goat has kicked your pail across the room for the third time or has just stepped into the pail, and you are thinking to yourself, "Now I see where that expression 'don't cry over spilled milk' comes from," remember that this too will pass, and that if you keep at it, one day you and your goat will find milking to be a happy, peaceful, and rewarding experience.

THE MILKING PROCESS: STEP BY STEP

To begin milking, pour a small bit of your goat's concentrate (if using) into her bowl, and get her to jump up onto the milking stand. Once her head's in place, lock the stanchion and get ready to milk.

Use one of your two soapy cloths to gently wash the teats and surrounding belly and udder. This is important both for the sake of your goat (who can get mastitis from dirt getting into the orifice of the teat) and for you. You want to minimize the amount of dirt and hair from the underside of the goat that falls into the milking pail.

Squirt a few jets of milk from each teat into your strip cup. If it looks clean and has no lumps, you are good to go. If it looks bloody or stringy, your goat probably has mastitis. Many feed stores carry mastitis test kits that are easy to use. All you need is milk from the goat in question. These tests work well and are good to have on hand. However, if your goat does have problems with her milk, it's best to get her to a vet as soon as possible for treatment, usually a course of antibiotics. Nursing human mothers can get mastitis too, and if you ask someone who has had it, you will learn that it can be painful.

Begin milking. If your goat has a tendency to kick, empty the pail every few cups so that she won't be spilling all the milk if she kicks the pail over towards the end. When you empty the pail, pour the milk through the strainer and filter into the milk jar.

When you're finished milking, clean the teats again with your second soapy, wet cloth, and then spray the teats with teat spray. This step of cleaning the teats and then spraying with teat spray is very important for the prevention of mastitis.

Clean your equipment. It is extremely important that you carefully clean your milking equipment after every use. Good sanitation will reduce your chance of disease and will help prevent off-tasting milk. Contaminated milk can develop a gamy flavor very quickly. I don't boil my milking equipment, but I always make sure to clean it right away. To clean your milking equipment, you can use the same system you use to clean your dinner dishes—that is, either run everything through a dishwasher or use standard dish soap and hot water in the sink.

ICE BATH FOR YOUR MILK

If you choose not to pasteurize your milk (a process described in the next section), as soon as you've finished milking and before beginning your other chores, you should place your jar of milk in a bucket, surround it with ice, add water, and place the chilling milk in your refrigerator. You can sometimes find ice buckets intended for chilling wine that work well for this. Alternatively, you can use a tall pot. Instead of using ice, you can also take a few plastic water bottles and freeze them. Tuck these frozen bottles of ice around your milk bottle, and then add water to the bucket. This method allows you to dispense with the need to fill ice cube trays every day. The idea of the ice water bath is to bring the temperature of the milk down to 33 to 39 degrees F as quickly as possible. This helps ensure a fresh taste and minimizes the potential for the growth of harmful bacteria. If you want to be really serious about chilling your milk quickly, put the mason jar in an ice bath even before you begin milking. This way, your milk will begin chilling as soon as it hits the jar.

Although you don't need to do it every day, at some point you should use a thermometer to check your milk to see how quickly it is chilling. If it is taking more than an hour to reach 39 degrees, you'll want to improve your cooling system.

If you do choose to pasteurize your milk, follow the instructions in the next section before chilling it.

How to Pasteurize Your Milk

To pasteurize your milk, heat it to 160 degrees F for thirty seconds or take it up to 140 degrees F and hold it there for thirty minutes. Then bring it down to a temperature of 39 degrees F as quickly as possible. You can use a standard candy thermometer, but if you are going to get serious about cheese making, consider a floating dairy thermometer or better yet a digital thermometer that will beep when it hits your specified temperature.

You can pasteurize the milk in a regular kitchen pot, set directly on a burner. However, if you use a double boiler, you'll be less likely to scald the milk, and you can also pour the hot water out of the bottom and replace it with ice water once the milk is up to temperature. This gets the milk cool enough to put into a glass bottle in an ice bath. A regular double boiler probably won't be big enough for your needs, so if you will be pasteurizing your milk regularly it's worth investing in a stovetop cheese vat. These are large (3- to 5-gallon) double boilers, available through cheese-making or goat supply catalogs. See Goaty Resources for sources. Rapid cooling can be done with an ice bath, as described in the previous section, but be sure to have the milk in a metal container. I found out the hard way that if you put hot milk into a glass bottle and then plunge the bottle into ice water, it will crack, and your milk will spill all over your kitchen counter and floor.

PASTEURIZATION VS. RAW MILK

Today, pasteurization is a hot topic. There are those who say it's a food safety no-brainer and others who claim that the benefits of raw milk outweigh the risks. Whatever you decide to do, know that selling or even giving away your milk has liability issues.

The main concern of health departments today is *E. coli* 0157. This bacterium has left some people paralyzed for life and killed others. It is the *E. coli* of the famous Jack-in-the-Box contamination fiasco and the Odwalla juice outbreak. It is also the *E. coli* that killed the young boy featured in the movie *Food, Inc*. Fortunately, while *E. coli* 0157 can prove deadly, it is not commonly found in goat milk. Other diseases that can be contracted from goat milk include listeriosis and Q fever—neither of which you want to get.

In researching the issue of pasteurization, I found it extremely difficult to find information that was truly science based and uninfluenced by general philosophy. For example, what are the actual risks of contracting *E. coli* from milk, in terms of percentages? Is goat milk less likely to be contaminated than cow milk?

The Seattle law firm of Marler Clark, famous for its work on food contamination litigation on behalf of consumers, has put together a website regarding the issue of pasteurization, www.realrawmilkfacts.com. Although the website argues against *purchasing* raw milk, it does include these two questions and answers that are helpful in deciding whether to pasteurize the goat milk you bring in from your backyard:

Is drinking raw milk directly from the farm safer?

Many people who grew up on a farm drank raw milk from their animals and do not recall ever getting sick. Does this mean drinking raw milk directly from the farm is safer?

It is true that farm families often drink their own raw milk and usually do not become sick. There is some scientific evidence that they develop immunity to the germs their animals carry. This is not necessarily true for people who don't live on a farm. Some of the most serious illnesses from raw milk over the last few years have been in adults and children who tried raw milk for the first time. The fact that the farmer and his/her children did not get sick does not mean that the milk is safe for people in the general population, especially if the milk is intended for pasteurization and not licensed and inspected as a Grade A raw dairy. Children, pregnant women, and people with immune system problems and chronic illnesses are at the highest risk

There is something very satisfying about carrying fresh milk in from your backyard. It is a thing of beauty.

of developing severe illness from contaminated raw dairy products, whether they are from a farm or a grocery store.

Is raw goat milk safer than cow milk?

There is no evidence that raw milk is safer from a particular species of animal. Goats may be easier to keep clean because they produce less manure than cows and a goat's fecal material is firmer and less likely to splash compared to that of cows, which have liquid feces. But people have been sickened by both goat and cow milk.

In 2008, a young boy and girl became severely ill after drinking raw goat milk contaminated with *E. coli* O157:H7 from a farm in Missouri.

Freedom from Milking

Everyone needs a backup milker. You may want to go on a short vacation, have plans for a late night out, or get injured or sick. It's best to find a backup milker who lives near you. If your backup has to milk both morning and evening, even a short commute will become burdensome.

Finding a backup milker is much harder than finding a cat sitter. While part of the problem is that the milking process takes time, the main problem is that learning to milk well enough to empty your goat's udder takes practice. I have had many people offer to milk for me, but when they came for their first practice session and realized it was a skill that would take time to learn, they bowed out. On the other hand, I've been surprised by how much some people enjoy milking and how excited they are to practice and learn. Because milkers can bow out at the last minute, and because learning to milk takes time, make sure to leave plenty of time to find and train your backup. Even if a person has experience milking, every goat is slightly different and you will want to make sure your backup milker knows how to milk *your* goat before you are out of cell phone range. Lastly, when training your backup, have patience and try to remember how it felt when you were learning to milk.

Some people have goat-milking apprentices. These people come once or twice a week to milk the goats, and in return they get to keep all or a portion of that day's milk. The apprentice system gives goat owners the benefit of a day off now and again and gives the apprentices the benefit of fresh milk without the daily cost and expense of keeping goats themselves.

Cheesemaking

By turning milk into cheese, people in the days before refrigeration were able to enjoy their milk, albeit in a different form, months after they'd milked it (nine months in the case of Parmesan). This was especially handy since dairy animals give milk according to the lactation curve — giving gallons in the spring and then slowly decreasing their production to just a trickle in the fall and winter. You too will face this problem of too much milk during the spring and too little in the winter. Making aged cheeses is tricky, but you can make soft chèvre and mozzarella with relative ease and freeze them. When defrosted, they'll taste very close to as good as they did on the day you made them. If you want to get really serious about cheese making, you can try your hand at hard cheeses like cheddar and Parmesan.

A two-day old Rosie Fluffy Socks contemplates taking a nap.

Making Mozzarella

This recipe makes almost a pound of mozzarella and should take an hour to an hour and a half. Making mozzarella is trickier than making chèvre, but it is more gratifying. You'll get to watch everyday milk transformed into a remarkably elastic and glossy mass that you will stretch and fold into truly delicious mozzarella. The key to making mozzarella is the acidity of the milk. You will increase your milk's acidity by adding citric acid, but the amount of citric acid you need to add will depend on your milk. That's why you need to use pH test paper. This may sound intimidating and bring back bad memories of chemistry lab, but pH test paper is easy to use and will help prevent you from ending up with a funny-looking mozzarella-like blob.

Once you've gathered together all the ingredients and equipment, you're ready to roll. Have fun and don't worry. Even if you mess up, what you'll end up with should taste good (even if it doesn't look good).

INGREDIENTS AND EQUIPMENT

1 gallon cold whole milk, or start with fresh, warm milk from the udder (You can use pasteurized or unpasteurized milk, but you cannot use *ultra*pasteurized milk, which today is just about any milk you find at the grocery store. You'll need to go to a food co-op or specialty grocery like Whole Foods to find milk that is not ultrapasteurized.)

1½ teaspoons citric acid dissolved in ¼ cup warm water (You may need a little more, according to your pH test.)

¼ tablet dry rennet dissolved in 2 tablespoons cool tap water for a few minutes, or ½ teaspoon liquid rennet

Salt

Stainless steel pot that can comfortably hold a gallon of milk. An enameled cast iron pot will work well too. Do not use aluminum kettles or utensils.

Long stainless steel spoon

pH test paper that will give you detailed readings for between 5 and 6.5 or thereabouts (available at home brew shops). You must be able to identify the range between 5 and 5.4. If you have a digital pH tester, all the better.

Thermometer

Long knife

Colander

Clean rubber dishwashing gloves

PROCESS

Pour the milk into the stainless steel pot and place over medium heat. Stir in the dissolved citric acid. Wait several minutes to allow the acidity of the milk to mix thoroughly and then check to see if the pH is between 5.0 and 5.4. If the pH number is 5.4 or above, stir in ¼ teaspoon more citric acid (dissolved in 2 tablespoons warm water). Wait a few minutes and test the pH again. If the pH is less than 5.0 (very unlikely), you're in trouble. Set the milk aside for drinking and start again using less citric acid. (Note: The higher the pH number, the lower the acidity.)

Heat the milk to 90 degrees F over low heat, stirring regularly to keep it from scorching. If after 15 minutes, the milk still hasn't reached 90 degrees, turn up the heat slightly.

Once the milk has reached 90 degrees F (it's okay if you overshoot a little and hit 100 degrees), add the rennet. Thoroughly but gently stir the rennet into the warm milk for 30 seconds with an up-and-down motion as well as an around-the-pot motion.

Let set for 15 minutes.

Cut the curd mass into ½-inch pieces. To do this, use a long knife to make a row of cuts from the surface of the curd all the way to the bottom of the pot, ½ inch apart. Do this again at a right angle to the first cuts so that you create a grid of cuts. Then hold the knife at a 45-degree angle and make a series of diagonal cuts. Turn the pot 90 degrees and do this again. The idea is to cut the curd into something approximating ½-inch by ½-inch by ½-inch pieces. (See photo.) Don't worry about being exact.

As soon as you have finished cutting, you'll want to hold the curds and whey at 90 degrees F for about 15 minutes, stirring gently now and again. The stirring equalizes the temperature in the pot and prevents scorching. The stirring motion is more like a fold, turn, or lift. The curds are fragile and can shatter, so use a gentle hand. To hold the temperature at 90 degrees, you may need to put the pot back over low heat once or twice. Some stoves have a warming plate. If you have one, use it for this stage.

Cut the curds with a long knife. The goal is to end up with cube-like pieces.

To separate the curds and whey, ladle or pour them into a colander. If you don't have cheesecloth, you can use a piece of old sheet that you have boiled for about 10 minutes. If you want to keep the whey, make sure to put a collection pot or bowl under the colander. You can feed the whey to your dog, chickens, or neighborhood body builder.

Gently stir the curds within the colander for a few minutes. The whey will slowly seep from the curds and escape.

Scoop 1 cup of the curds into a Pyrex measuring cup. Add ½ teaspoon salt (this amount can vary depending on how salty you like your cheese), and stir it in with a spoon. Place the cup of curds in the microwave, and heat on high power for 1 minute.

The curds are very hot when they come out of the microwave, so use rubber gloves for the next step. Remove the very hot curds from the microwave and, over a colander (to catch any curds you may drop), massage them with your hands, squeezing out the whey and mixing it. Parts of the mass will be warmer than others. The idea is to mix the wad of curd to disperse the heat and release the whey. After about 30 seconds of this, try stretching the mass by pulling it apart with your hands. Then fold it back into a mass and stretch it again. If you've got a good stretch, you'll be able to pull the cheese a foot or more apart without breaking it. Continue to stretch and fold until the cheese begins to harden and lose its stretch. If you don't get a stretch, try microwaving the curd for another 30 seconds and then massaging and stretching it again.

Form the stretched mozzarella into a ball and pop it into a bowl of ice water or cold whey.

Repeat the final three steps with the remaining curds.

Sometimes, for reasons I don't understand, the cheese doesn't stretch and ends up as a hard blob. This is a little disappointing, but don't throw it out. It will still taste good and will work well on pizza.

Freeze what you don't plan to eat within a week. If left to sit in the refrigerator for more than a week, the cheese can take on a gamy flavor.

This recipe makes a very mild-tasting mozzarella. If you want more flavor, add 1 tablespoon yogurt containing live cultures at the same time that you add the citric acid.

Making Chèvre

Chèvre is one of the easiest cheeses to make. It's relatively foolproof and provides a good yield (about 3 cups of cheese per gallon of milk). If you don't have enough milk from your own goats, you can use storebought pasteurized milk, but ultrapasteurized milk will not work. Ultrapasteurization is not the same as pasteurization. Usually, but not always, if milk has been ultrapasteurized, it will say so on the carton. Today, almost all large-scale dairies ultrapasteurize.

Whether you use pasteurized or raw milk is up to you. Both work well. Do keep in mind that you will be creating the perfect environment for microbial growth—warmth, moisture, and nutrients (the milk). This means that if any pathogenic bacteria happen to be present in your milk, they will multiply rapidly. E. coli doubles its population every twenty minutes under optimal conditions such as those required to make chèvre.

INGREDIENTS AND EQUIPMENT

1 gallon goat milk (remember, if you buy it from the store, make sure it is not ultrapasteurized)

1 packet chèvre starter (this contains a mesophilic cheese culture and a touch of rennet) or ½ cup buttermilk (a type of mesophilic culture) and 2 drops liquid rennet dissolved in ¼ cup water (see the Goaty Resources section)

4 teaspoons salt (more or less to taste)

Stainless steel or enameled cast iron pot that can comfortably hold a gallon of milk

Long stainless steel spoon for stirring

Colander

Piece of cheesecloth about 24 by 24 inches. You can use storebought cheesecloth or take a clean old sheet, cut it into squares, boil all the pieces for 10 minutes, and then hang them to dry.

Thermometer (the digital ones that beep when the milk has attained the specified temperature are worth every penny)

PROCESS

Heat the milk to 80 degrees F in a large stainless steel pot.

Stir in the chèvre starter packet or buttermilk and diluted rennet.

Remove from the heat and let sit for 8 to 12 hours. If you can, it's best to keep the temperature between 65 and 85 degrees F.

Pour curds and whey into a colander lined with cheesecloth. Bring the four corners of the cheesecloth together and tie closed at the top. Hang the bundle for twelve hours allowing the whey to drain slowly.

When the 8 to 12 hours are up, you'll find that the milk has transformed and is now a yogurtlike white substance (the curds) surrounded by a yellow translucent substance (the whey). Line a colander with a piece of cheesecloth, and pour in the curds and whey. If you want to save the whey, put a pot under the colander to capture it. Stir the curds and whey around for a few minutes to help the whey drain.

Add salt to taste and stir (try 4 teaspoons for your first batch).

Gather together the four corners of the cheesecloth and hold for a minute or two to let more whey drain.

Tie a string around the cheesecloth and hang the bundle. Put a pot beneath the bundle.

Allow the bundle to hang for 12 hours. You'll be surprised by the amount of whey that drips into the capture pot.

Cut down the bundle, open the cheesecloth, and cut the cheese into sections. The section size depends on how much cheese you like to eat in a week. Wrap the sections in plastic wrap and freeze what you won't be eating that week.

If you want, you can shape your chèvre into balls or logs for a distinguished look.

That's it. Enjoy!

Rosie pulls hay down from her manger.

The more time you spend with your goats, the more likely you'll be to notice if one becomes ill.

CHAPTER TWELVE

GOAT HEALTH CARE

MANY BOOKS GO INTO GREAT DETAIL ON HOW to neuter and disbud and how to diagnose and treat your goats with medicines purchased from the feed store or folk remedies available though the Internet. This is not one of those books. But it just may be that it will serve you better than those others, because when you are starting out with goat keeping, you shouldn't really be diagnosing and treating anyway. You are going to need to pay professionals to help you and learn as you go. What you need to know when starting out is how to find the right professional to help you help your goat. You also need to know about hoof trimming, dewormers, and the need to keep a careful eye on your goat's health. As a prey animal, if your goat is feeling under the weather, she will do all she can to hide her sickness from the world.

The Nature of Goat Vets and How to Choose One

The trouble with goat vets is that there is really no such thing. Even out in the country, there just aren't that many goats. Most large-animal vets see goats now and again, but horses and cows are their real bread and butter, with goats making up perhaps 5 percent of their practice at best. There's also relatively little medical research pertaining to goats. Such research simply does not pay. Therefore, although large-animal vets can save your goats from an array of diseases and disorders, and there will be times that your goats will desperately need one, you may notice that these vets are not as proficient as dog and cat vets. They can't be. There simply aren't enough goats out there for them to get experience from, and there isn't enough research for them to review.

While it is hard to find a good goat vet out in the country, it is even harder to find one in the city. However, if you call around, you may just get lucky. Here in Seattle, there's a wonderful goat vet who spent years working with goats and horses in the Midwest before settling down to a simpler life of treating dogs and cats delivered to him in the warm waiting room of a clinic.

If you have several goat vets to choose from, talk with other experienced goat owners to find out who they like. Also talk to the vet and find out how much experience he or she has with goats. See if you can find out approximately how many goats they see on average in a month or year.

Who Will Disbud Her or Neuter Him?

When it comes time to neuter one of your new bucklings or disbud your kids, you can go to a vet or an experienced goat keeper. Oddly enough, many goat keepers are more experienced with disbudding and neutering than some vets. Often cooperative extension services can connect you with experienced goat keepers who are skilled at these two procedures. If you want to assess those who are recommended, read up on the procedure you would like done and then talk with the person you are thinking of hiring to find out how familiar they are with the basics. The Goaty Resources section at the end of the book contains a web address for a US Department of Agriculture list of cooperative extension services.

DISBUDDING

Whatever you do, be sure to decide who will take care of disbudding your kids before your goat gives birth, as it needs to be done before they are a week old. When goats are born they have no horns, just little horn buds. These grow quickly, and by the time the kid is four days old, the buds are about the size of chocolate chips. Disbudding prevents a goat from growing horns, and involves burning off the horn buds with a special type of red-hot iron. Once a goat has grown horns, they are extremely difficult to remove, due to the way they are connected to the skull.

Although it is physically possible to disbud a day-old kid, you should wait until it is at least three days old to allow it to recover from birthing and gain some strength and stability. If you wait more than a week to disbud, however, the procedure will become more difficult and your goat could develop scurs (bits of malformed horns that grow). Scurs are really hard to remove. Don't wait.

Note that Nigerian Dwarves have far hardier horn buds than do standard dairy breeds. Therefore, the disbudding procedure is different and more intense with Nigerians and Nigerian crosses (minis). In disbudding a Nigerian or a mini, you need to burn the scalp even more, going all the way to the cartilage, as opposed to the less deep and intense "copper ring stage." If you disbud a Nigerian or mini-goat kid by just burning through to the copper ring stage, your goat will get scurs. With standard dairy breeds, you shouldn't have this problem. When interviewing a person about disbudding your kids, get a feel for whether they know about the different requirements of Nigerians. If they don't, and you have a Nigerian or mini, keep looking.

NEUTERING

Neutering is best done when bucklings are between six and twelve weeks of age. Neutering before six weeks can interfere with the full development of the urethra. This in turn can lead to the buildup of urinary calculi, a painful and often deadly condition. Bucklings can become fertile as young as three months old, and you do not want a young buckling impregnating his mother and aunts. Hence, the six- to twelve-week window.

You may be tempted to neuter your bucklings before they reach six weeks of age, due to their extreme dedication to their future job as inseminators. Bucklings begin practicing for "their work" at just a few days of age, with great enthusiasm and dedication. They will practice on their brothers, your leg, their sisters, the watering can—anything and everything. While their behavior may seem inappropriate and irk you, don't succumb to the temptation to neuter early. It could harm their health and also doesn't help curb their appetite for "practicing." You must learn to accept that bucklings will be bucklings.

To choose who will neuter your bucklings, you need to know that there are three main methods:

- **The surgical method,** in which an incision is made and the testicles are cut out

- **The Burdizzo method,** which requires no cutting but instead crushes the spermatic cord, thereby cutting off the blood supply to the scrotum and thus destroying the testicles

- **The elastrator method,** also known as banding. In this method, a specially designed elastic band is put around the scrotum just above the testes. The band is left on, and within two weeks, the testes and scrotum fall off.

Many people believe that the elastrator method is the least humane of the three methods, so if you have an option, it's best to opt for the Burdizzo or surgical method. Laura Workman, my goat mentor, has tried all three methods and has come to strongly prefer the Burdizzo method. According to her, it is effective, the least painful, and the least likely to become infected.

Trimming Hooves

Goats in the wild do not need hoof trimming because they naturally file down their hooves by climbing around on rocks all day. Not so with city goats, who while away the hours stepping over a soft bed of wood chips. Dentists will often tell you that healthy teeth are necessary for overall good health. This is true of hoof health too. Untrimmed goat hooves are prone to a bacterial disease called hoof rot that can lead to systemic illness. Untrimmed hooves can also effectively cripple a goat. Therefore, it's important to take good care of your goat's hooves through regular trimming.

It's best to trim goat hooves every month, cutting off small amounts each time, rather than waiting several months and having to cut more at once. This is especially true in the winter, when you will be fighting off mud with wood chips and will inevitably lose a few battles.

If you can, find someone to demonstrate hoof trimming before you try to do it yourself. If you can remember, ask the person you are buying your goats from to show you how when you pick up the goats to bring them home. There is also an excellent DVD available on the topic (see Goaty Resources).

Use your milking stand to help hold your goat still while you trim her hooves.

Another option is to hire a farrier. Farriers make their living tending to and shoeing horses, but many also work with goats.

Goat hooves are unlike dog nails or human fingernails. Around the edge, they have a nail-like substance that grows relatively quickly. This part is called the wall. Inside the wall is the sole. The sole section also needs trimming. The sole is not flesh, as in muscle, but it's not like a typical fingernail either; it's a sort of amalgamation of the two, but it doesn't hurt when you cut it. In many ways, the sole is like an incredibly thick callus.

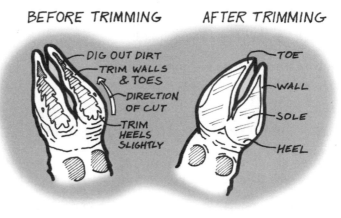

BEFORE TRIMMING

- DIG OUT DIRT
- TRIM WALLS & TOES
- DIRECTION OF CUT
- TRIM HEELS SLIGHTLY

AFTER TRIMMING

- TOE
- WALL
- SOLE
- HEEL

Views of hoof bottom

To trim goat hooves, you'll need:

- ❧ Trimming shears

- ❧ Sanitizing solution for the trimmers when you are through

- ❧ Styptic powder to stop the flow of blood in the event that you cut too far

- ❧ Hoof brush and pick

If you have thick gloves that fit well enough to allow you to maneuver your fingers with precision, use them. They can protect your hands should the shears slip. For trimming shears, you can make do with a good-quality pair of garden shears, but the ones sold specifically for goat hooves work best. These are available from the goat supply catalogs (see Goaty Resources), as are styptic powder, hoof brushes, and hoof picks.

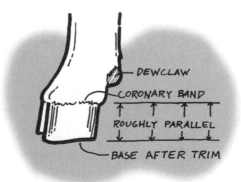

- DEWCLAW
- CORONARY BAND
- ROUGHLY PARALLEL
- BASE AFTER TRIM

Side view after trimming

To trim your goat's hooves:

1. **Lock her into her milking stand.**

2. **Brush and scrape the hooves clean.** A clean hoof allows you to see clearly what you are doing.

In cutting, your goal is to make the front part of the hoof the same height as the back part. In other words, you want the coronary band (see illustration) to be parallel to the ground when the goat is standing.

3. **Begin by trimming the wall,** cutting it so that it no longer extends beyond the sole.

4. **Then trim the sole** by cutting off flakes from front to back. As you cut off flakes, you'll soon notice that the sole underneath looks pink. Don't cut below the pink or your goat will begin to bleed. If your goat does bleed, pat styptic powder on it and be more careful with the next hoof. You may notice a few small (⅛ or less) bubbles in the sole. These are a very early stage of hoof rot. If possible, cut them out. If cutting them out would cause bleeding, just open the bubbles up to expose them to air.

Off Her Feed

Goats hide their illnesses much better than cats or dogs because they are prey animals. Their wild ancestors could not afford to show weakness. Also, the digestive system of a goat relies on a healthy population of bacteria. If this population falters, life-threatening problems can develop extremely quickly.

A sure sign of a problem with the bacterial population of the rumen is a loss of appetite. If a goat goes off her feed, she may well have a serious problem and should be taken to the vet immediately. This is especially true if she's been getting grain and has lost interest in it. It's a good idea, before you call your vet, to have as much information

BRUSHING

Many goats enjoy being brushed. Brushing your goats is a nice way to spend some quality time with them, helps keep them looking glamorous, and is even good for their health by helping to keep external parasites at bay. Both curry combs (horse brushes) and FURminators (a popular brand of dog and cat brush) work well for goat grooming and are available through most pet supply shops and feed stores.

handy as possible. Take your goat's temperature (by placing the thermometer in her rectum while she is locked in the milking stand). A normal goat temperature is 102 to 103 degrees F. Also check the rumen by listening to the left side of your goat's flanks and counting the number of rumblings you hear in a minute. Fewer than three rumblings in a minute requires urgent care.

Worms

During your time as a goat keeper you will inevitably encounter internal parasites in the form of worms. There are many types of these pests—roundworms, pinworms, and strongyle worms to name just a few. A number of products are available to treat these internal parasites. The two main ones are:

- ❡ **Ivermectin,** sold in injectable, pour-on, and oral form (the oral form is preferred and is sold at feed stores in tubes marketed for horses). Ivermectin should be dosed at twice the dosage recommended for horses or cattle on a per pound basis.

- ❡ **Fenbendazole,** sold as Safe-Guard for goats (available at feed stores and through goat supply catalogs).

Both of these dewormers can be incredibly effective. However, just as antibiotics can foster the evolution of antibiotic-resistant bacteria, dewormers can foster the evolution of dewormer-resistant worms. In using a dewormer, don't try to play it safe and underdose. If you do, you'll allow worms that can tolerate low doses of the dewormer to live and reproduce. In certain parts of the country, ivermectin is no longer effective due to overuse and improper use. Thus, use chemical dewormers with educated caution. Never treat your goat with a dewormer unless you are sure she actually has worms. To make sure, have a fecal test done on her. This involves taking a few of her fresh pellets to a vet for examination. The vet will turn her pellets into a slurry and view them under a high-power microscope in a search for offending parasites. If the vet finds worms, you should deworm according to his or her instructions.

IMPORTANT EXCEPTION TO THE DEWORMER RULE

The one exception to this rule is just after your goat has given birth. After kidding, a goat is so exhausted that any small worm problem she may have (and she likely has a mild one) will blossom and grow. Nip this in the bud by dosing her with a dewormer within twelve hours after she kids. In all other instances, have a fecal sample done before breaking out the big antiworm guns.

Although Maple used to sometimes chase chickens for sport and even nipped at them, she never hurt them.

GOATS AND YOUR FAMILY

MANY PEOPLE WHO KEEP GOATS KEEP OTHER ANIMALS AS WELL. Here's what's important to know about the dynamics between goats and your other pets or family members.

Goats and Chickens

Is it right for chickens and goats to cohabitate?

Chickens and goats can live together peaceably with no damage done to their mental, spiritual, or physical health. However, as is always the case with chickens, their feed attracts rats. Goat concentrate (goat chow) attracts rats too, but because goats wolf it down readily without leaving a crumb, the keeping of goats does not attract rats. Chickens, on the other hand, peck at their food a bit here and a bit there all day long.

Another problem with chickens sharing a yard with goats is that goats are attracted to chicken feed, and chicken feed can be lethal to goats. If you are using one of those chicken feeders that allow you to set out a whole gallon of chicken feed, and if the goats get into that feeder when it is anywhere near full, your goats may well eat themselves to death. The richness of the chicken feed messes with the bacteria balance in the rumen, which in turn can lead to a deadly disease called enterotoxaemia.

To prevent rats and goats from getting access to chicken feed, you can simply lock the chicken feed in a rat- and goat-proof chicken coop. By doing this, you'll be locking the chicken feed away from the chickens during the day, but they'll have from dusk until dawn to eat. During the day, when the chickens are locked out of their coop and don't have access to their feed, they can forage for bugs and bits of foliage that fall from

Spencer holds Snowflake's daughter, Flora.

the goats' foliage feeder (which happens all day long). Since your coop holds the chickens for only twelve hours, it need not be deluxe. You can make a simple rat-proof coop using an old kitchen cabinet. These are available in a huge assortment of sizes and shapes at building salvage shops. Most are quite reasonably priced.

To convert a kitchen cabinet into a coop, you'll need to put a latch on the door and cut some holes and cover them with hardware cloth for ventilation. If you add a trap door to the bottom of the cabinet and set the coop on legs, cleanup is easy. Fill the bottom with wood shavings every week, and then at the end of the week open the trap door, brush the wood shavings and poop into a bucket, and add clean wood shavings.

This method of using a retrofitted kitchen cabinet for a coop does require that you provide your hens with nesting boxes for use during the day. It's best to place these nesting boxes out of reach of the goats, so that they don't put their noses in and bother the chickens while the chickens are laying. I once had a goat, Maple, who ate chicken eggs. I was convinced that my hens were shirking their egg-laying duties because it was spring and I was getting very few eggs. However, just before I decided to retire them to the great chicken coop in the sky, I discovered that they were, in fact, quite dedicated to their egg laying duties. The problem was that they were laying a large percentage of their eggs on the floor of the goat shed, and Maple was right behind them as they did so, gobbling up their new creations. My son, Spencer, is the one who figured this out. One day he was out collecting eggs from the coop. He took the eggs out one at a time and set them on the ground. When he turned around to set down the last egg, there was Maple beside him, egg dripping from her mouth. When he looked for the eggs he'd set down, they were gone.

The biggest downside to having chickens in your goat area is chicken poop. Every once in a while, a chicken will poop on your milking stand, and if you don't put a lid on your hay manger, they'll get in it to lay eggs and poop there too. Rarely, maybe twice a year or so, and this depends on the chicken, they will hop onto a goat's back and poop. This is no fun to clean up.

You may worry that chickens will pass strongyle worms or some other type of parasites on to your goats, because both goats and chickens can get strongyle worms (these are especially disgusting long, stringy worms). However, this need not concern you. According to my veterinarian, most parasites are species specific, and while both chickens and goats can get strongyle worms, they are each getting a different type of strongyle worm and cannot pass them from one to another.

GUARD GOATS

With the exception of the occasional emotionally disturbed dog, goats have no predators in cities and suburbs. The same can't be said for chickens. I've found, however, that goats are actually good guard animals for chickens. Although I have seen raccoons just yards from my goat yard's fence line, no raccoon has ever taken one of my hens.

Eddie-the-Pug and Eloise-the-Kid are curious about one another, but are not close friends.
(Photo by Lori Eanes)

I do generally lock my hens in a raccoon-proof coop at night, but many nights, I have forgotten to do this, and still no harm has come to my hens.

Seattle has wandering coyotes, and a coyote attacked and killed a raccoon in my neighborhood. However, coyotes are not numerous enough (yet) in cities to form packs and kill goats. Such is not the case in the country, where coyotes have attacked goats who didn't have the security of a sturdy fence and the nighttime protection of a well-built goat shed. Cougars also can and do kill and eat goats in rural areas.

Goats and Cats or Dogs

Sometimes, cats hang around near my goat yard, but they never go into it. They seem to enjoy sitting just outside the fence on sunny days, twitching their tails and watching whatever the chickens and goats are up to. Maybe they are hunting rats.

How your goats and dog get along depends very much on the dog and somewhat on the goats. Dogs have been known to kill goats, yet many dogs happily run in and out of their farm's goat yard without upset. I've even seen a picture of a goat and dog snuggled up together. The key is not to leave goats and dogs without supervision until you have a good sense of how they get along. When introducing your dog, keep it on a leash so that if it becomes aggressive, you can pull it away. Be aware that some dogs will attack with little warning. Certain breeds, such as the Anatolian shepherd and Great Pyrenees, have been bred specifically to guard livestock and are predisposed to be good with goats.

One problem with allowing dogs into the goat/chicken yard is that many dogs have a nasty habit of eating goat and chicken poop. The various pugs I have owned or fostered over the years have all done this, so either pugs have especially disgusting taste or there's something about goat and chicken poop that many dogs find appealing.

Goats and Children

Goats and children can get along fabulously, or not. Snowflake doesn't do well with children. She likes to scare strangers by rearing up and waving her two front hooves about in a menacing manner like a wild mustang. Large people who are comfortable around goats tell her to buzz off when she does this. They'll give her a shove and call her a bossy broad right to her face. Children, on the other hand, become truly terrified. Some goats, like Maple, are gentle and quiet and can be trusted to gently nuzzle children and refrain from butting them, even when they bend over and provide a tempting target.

Just as some goats cannot be trusted around children, some children cannot be trusted around goats. Some young children have been known to try to ride a goat like a

There's a good reason why both young children and goats are called kids.

horse. Others can be trusted to always be gentle and kind to goats and hold their own if a goat gets rowdy. Children as young as ten can even learn to be proficient milkers. Almost all children find goats interesting and will enjoy watching you milk and want to give it a try.

Camping with Your Goat

One of the downsides of keeping goats is that it is tough to leave town if they are in milk. A solution to this dilemma is to take your goats with you on your trip. They won't like a very long car ride, but a ride of a few to several hours won't do them any harm. Because most hotels don't allow goats in their rooms, and most of your friends will get angry with you if you bring a goat into their homes, you will need to take up camping. The upside of camping with dairy goats is that you don't need to bring milk.

Donna Semasko of Edelweiss Acres, a goat-packing outfit in Olympia, Washington, has been packing with goats for many years and kindly took the time to answer some of my questions about camping with goats. Here's what I found.

How do you keep your goats safe at night?

We use a horse line. We tie a rope between two trees and pull it tight. It should be about 4 feet from the ground. Then we hook the goats to a line attached to this line. It needs to be long enough to allow them to lie down, but not too long to allow them to get tangled in it.

How do you protect them from the rain?

We use a tarp that we hang above the goat line.

What about cougars, bears, wolves, and coyotes? Will they attack?

We have been camping for many years with goats and have even done so in country where there are grizzly bears. We've never had the goats attacked. It may be that the animals don't come around because we are right there in a tent next to the goats. It may also be that they don't know what to make of the goats and sense it is wise to stay away.

Where can I get goat-packing supplies?

Check out Northwest Pack Goats (www.northwestpackgoats.com) and Butt-Head Pack Goats (www.buttheadpackgoats.com).

Where can I find campsites and trails that permit goats?

Goats are not allowed in national parks, but they are often allowed in national forests, state forests, and some county parks, and it is not uncommon to see a goat enjoying a day hike on the trail. The Horse & Mule Trail Guide USA website (www.horseandmuletrails.com) is a great resource for finding trails and campgrounds in your state that allow horses (or in your case goats).

Is this doe dreaming of romantic love? Probably not; female goats dream of stud bucks only when they're in heat.

A GOAT LOVE STORY

GENERALLY, WHEN YOU BREED A DOE, you take her to the stud buck, and if she is in fact in heat, she will mate three times in thirty minutes and that is the end of the relationship. The miracle of life happens and baby goats enter the world, but the father and mother may never meet again. I am often saddened by this thought and have wondered what a doe/stud buck relationship would be like if they were allowed more time together. As it happens, I came to know.

One spring, I found myself with just one goat, Snowflake. Brownie had died suddenly and unexpectedly from what the vet thought, based on blood work, was a ruptured bladder. The vet said this sometimes just happens. While I grieved for Brownie, I worried about Snowflake. I desperately hoped she was pregnant. I had bred her in the fall, and if she were to give birth, she'd have her own two kids to keep her company. I could have gone out and bought her a companion goat, but she is a persnickety sort of goat, and I worried she might not like the newcomer. Snowflake would definitely be happiest if she had her own kids.

Since I couldn't be sure that Snowflake was pregnant, I took her to the vet for a blood draw and mailed the blood sample to BioTracking. They do pregnancy tests for goats. (They can also test to see if your bison or elk is pregnant for only $7). Ten days later, I got bad news. Snowflake was not pregnant.

It was early March, and goats typically go into heat only between September and February, give or take a month on either side. Given the time of year, it was uncertain whether Snowflake would go into heat again. I'd heard from a woman who kept a large herd of goats that her does were still cycling, so there was a chance things could work out. I figured since time was running out, I'd need Snowflake to live with a stud buck, so that if she did go into heat, I wouldn't miss it.

At the time, Laura Workman had a stud named Bosco who she'd been urging me to pair up with Snowflake. Bosco lived on Laura's farm with a flock of sheep who frequently bothered him by nibbling his coat. This gave him a disheveled look, but according to Laura he had great potential and would help Snowflake "throw" kids with fantastic udders and large teats. Given her enthusiasm for the match, I called her to see if Snowflake could stay at her place with Bosco until Snowflake's time was right and they consummated their relationship. This would save me the trouble of whisking Snowflake up to the farm on the spur of the moment. For whatever reason, it seemed to me that big trouble always arose whenever it was Snowflake's "time."

Unfortunately, Laura said she had too many kids on the ground for Snowflake to stay with her. It was then that I had an idea. I asked, "Could Bosco come stay here with Snowflake?"

Laura paused for a moment and then said, "Sure, I don't see why not." Bosco's schedule was pretty open, so I was able to pick him up on Sunday morning. You might be thinking, "But stud bucks do not belong in the city because they are so incredibly smelly." It turns out that they are smelly only during rutting season and that they don't get smelly until they are about a year old. Since it was the tail end of rutting season and Bosco was not a year old yet, this wasn't a problem. What about the legality of all this? I reasoned that Bosco would just be visiting, and if he did bother anyone, I would solve the problem by immediately returning him home.

That Sunday I drove to Laura's, picked Bosco up in the station wagon, and was quite excited when I pushed him through the gate into the goat yard. But I can't really say the same for Snowflake. The first thing she did was to butt him on the head—hard. He wasn't going to take that, so he started butting her, and the two ended up spending their whole first day together butting heads. I thought this was a poor start to a relationship, but you never know. I watched and waited.

The trouble started after Bosco had been living with Snowflake for about a week. The two had stopped butting heads, and while they slept together in the goat shed, they nestled down in opposite corners. Bosco was behaving well. He was quiet and not smelly, and didn't bother any neighbors. The trouble was all the grief I began to get from friends. Bosco was only eight months old and he was just two-thirds the size of Snowflake. He didn't yet look like a macho stud buck. If he were a movie star, he'd be like a young Michael J. Fox, not an older Gérard Depardieu. In some ways, I'd even say that he bordered on the effeminate. Anna's husband, Colin, said, when he saw Bosco,

"Isn't he going to need scaffolding or something?" My neighbor Emily from across the street said, "He's only eight months old? That's just wrong." Judy said, "Gosh, I didn't know Snowflake was a cougar," and Melissa said, "I just don't understand the mechanics of how that would work."

All this got me worried that Bosco wasn't up to the job, so I called Laura. She said I needed to have more faith in the little guy. And so I waited. Over those few weeks, time seemed to pass slowly, and as it did, I began to sense that Bosco and Snowflake were falling in love. Bosco took to nuzzling Snowflake, and when I took Snowflake to my upper yard for a photo shoot for the cheese magazine *Culture*, he got quite upset and did a lot of fussy and plaintive bleating. I could tell Snowflake liked him too. She would lie down right next to him in the goat shed. It was at about this time that I became convinced that Snowflake was pregnant. I never did see any "action," but if you watch a lot of Hollywood romantic comedies, you'll notice that the relationship between the hero and heroine *always* starts out with some serious head butting, then the hero and heroine grow fond of one another and, in the end, walk away into the sunset. Just before the credits, a kid then skips into view from over the crest of a hilltop and runs toward the camera. The head butting and growing fond of one another were Snowflake and Bosco to a T. So, being well versed in the Hollywood script, I fully expected goat kids to skip into view in September.

But sadly, real life is not the movies, and not only did Snowflake not get pregnant, but Bosco had to move away, back to the field he shared with a flock of sheep who liked to spend their days pulling out his hair. It was all really quite sad.

Fortunately for you, though, I do not write tragedies, and although this was the end of the chapter, it was not the end of the story. Laura found an even better stud buck than Bosco and sent Bosco to another farm, where he is free from the hair-pulling sheep and where his job is to mate with show goats. I'm told he has no complaints. Snowflake, too, moved on. In the fall following her springtime romance with Bosco, she came into heat and mated with Laura's upgraded stud buck, Captain Morgan, and five months later gave birth to two healthy kids—a son and a daughter. The son got a job working as part of the well-respected brush clearing outfit Rent-a-Ruminant. There he is well cared for and gets to hang out with the celebrity goats who starred in the Stephen Colbert exposé about goats stealing jobs from American landscapers. Eloise, Snowflake's daughter, has stayed with her mother. She and Snowflake have a close bond and can often be found, on warm spring afternoons, chewing their cud at the top of their goat yard stairs and relaxing in the sunshine, with their necks draped over one another.

ACKNOWLEDGMENTS

SPECIAL THANKS TO SEATTLE CITY COUNCIL MEMBER Richard Conlin and legislative aide Phyllis Schulman, for telling me, "We don't want to help you get a waiver to allow you to keep goats; we want to help *legalize* goats for everyone in Seattle." They risked much in their efforts, including a lot of people saying they were wasting their time working on "small" issues. Politicians do, of course, need to tackle difficult, big issues, but if they did this to the exclusion of the easy-to-solve small ones, what sort of country would we live in? Do we really want to hear a politician say, "Sorry, that's an easy problem to fix, but I can't help you. Your problem is *too small*."

Thanks to Snowflake for being such a fabulous mother and giving lots of rich and creamy milk. This I appreciate, even when she misbehaves (which is pretty frequently).

Thanks to my editor, Kate Rogers, who encouraged me and gave me the opportunity to write a book, but always, with great tenderness and kindness, kept my feet on the ground. Plus, she greatly improved my prose and rearranged awkward sentences when necessary.

Thanks to my senior editor, Mary Metz, who kept the whole process of creating this book running smoothly, skillfully corrected prose where needed, hunted down obscure goat photos from across the globe, cheered me up a time or two with her literary wit, and seemed to truly enjoy her crash course in all things goat.

Thanks to Harley Soltes for making so many trips to Seattle and taking such artful photos. Thanks also to those who provided "breed" photos: Ilene White Freedman of House in the Woods Farm, Rachel Anderson, Grace Lukens, Liz Dawson, Terri Nii, and Liz Lawley. Thanks to Charity Lynn for my author photo. For her photos of the goat yard, thanks to Lori Eanes, whose beautiful photography can be found at lorieanes .com.

Thanks to my fellow Skipstone writer, goat owner, and friend, Melany Vorass, for her encouragement along the way and for thinking up the remarkable over the kitchen window compost machine. Thanks too to Rachel Baker, for her edits and support early on in the process.

Thanks and love to my husband, Don Kneass, who told me to go for it and write a book, despite it taking a lot of time and not being an especially profitable venture. (But you can all prove him wrong by buying lots of copies of this book.)

Thanks to historian Fred Brown for his great interest in people and animals and his history of animals in Seattle. He started me thinking critically about the separation of pet and farm animal.

Thanks to Anne Mendelson for her fascinating book *Milk: The Surprising Story of Milk Through the Ages*. Her book has kept me foraging for blackberry bramble for my goats even after getting a lot of scratches on hot summer afternoons. Because my milk is worth it.

Thanks to Melissa and Tom Clauson of Total Creative, who spiffed up my logo so that no one would be able to resist buying a Goat Justice League T-shirt. They get additional special thanks for proving that there are people out there who get goats and love them so much that they never look back.

Thanks to my neighbors Judith Starbuck and Peter Greenfield for enjoying having goats next door. In addition, Peter's wisdom was a great help in the goat legalization campaign, and Judith came up with the original and whimsical illustration of the Caped Crusader Goat.

Thanks to Apprentice Milkers David Mackie, Bonnie Briggs, and Cora Trujillo for their enthusiasm about goats and milking. They buoyed my enthusiasm for goat keeping and enabled me to get away now and again.

Special thanks to Laura Workman of Glimmercroft Farm, who patiently, and not so patiently, taught me almost everything I know about dairy goats and, when necessary, reminds me of what I don't know. If Laura ever writes a goat book, you should buy it.

GLOSSARY

abomasum The fourth stomach of a goat, sometimes called the true stomach. This stomach is the only one that produces digestive enzymes. It is responsible for most of the digestion of grain and milk.

banding A method of castrating bucklings in which a thick band is placed at the top of the testicles.

beet pellets Dry pellets made from the by-products of beet sugar manufacturing. They are rich in fiber and tasty to goats.

berry bag A contraption that attaches to a goat and catches her poop before it falls to the ground. Functionally, a berry bag is a goat diaper, but berry bags appear more similar to the manure bags worn by horses in parades than to the nappies worn by human babies.

browse The leafy greens from bushes and trees that goats so enjoy.

buck A full-grown unneutered male goat. Goat enthusiasts prefer the word to billy, which they consider to be slightly derogatory.

buckling A male baby goat who has not been neutered.

buck rag A rag that has been rubbed all over a buck in rut. These specialty items smell like stud bucks and are used to help determine whether a doe is in heat.

bun bag A specific brand of berry bag and the only commercially available berry bag made for goats.

Burdizzo method A bloodless method of neutering a goat that involves crushing the spermatic cord with a tool called a Burdizzo.

clicker training An operant conditioning method of animal training that uses a clicker to mark or "bridge" a desired behavior.

colostrum A precursor to true milk. It is yellowish in color and rich in antibodies and minerals. It is produced only during the first few days following kidding.

concentrate A rich, nonfoliage food source given to goats during the last two months of pregnancy and throughout lactation. Generally it is made up of grain and a protein supplement such as soy meal.

coronary band The upper, almost circular limit of the hoof.

disbud A process of scalding a goat kid's horn buds with a disbudding iron to prevent the growth of horns.

doe A full-grown female goat. Goat enthusiasts now eschew the word nanny.

doeling A young female goat.

elastrator method See banding.

freshening Whenever a goat gives birth and begins to give milk, she is said to have freshened.

hobble A tool that connects the two back hooves of a goat and that is purported to force poorly behaved goats to stand still during milking.

hoof rot An infection of the hoof caused by anaerobic bacteria. Hoof rot can be prevented with monthly hoof trimming and by minimizing mud through proper drainage and the liberal use of wood chips.

lactation duration The period of time during which a goat continues to lactate.

manger A piece of farm equipment that contains and dispenses hay.

mastitis A bacterial infection of the mammary gland.

mineral mix A sort of goat vitamin best provided to goats in loose (nonblock) form.

milking stand A piece of farmyard furniture that helps ease the chore of milking by raising the goat up to a convenient height and holding her in position.

omasum The third stomach of a goat.

pasteurized milk Milk that has been heated to 140 degrees F for thirty minutes or 160 degrees F for five seconds in order to destroy microorganisms and prevent fermentation.

Pritchard nipple A type of nipple that attaches to soda-style bottles and is used to bottle-feed goat kids.

reticulum The second stomach of a goat.

roughage The part of a goat's diet made up of leaves, including the leaves of dried grass (hay).

rumen The first stomach of a goat and the primary fermentation tank of the goat digestive system.

settle A goat is said to have "settled" when she becomes pregnant.

scur A partial horn that grows if disbudding isn't done perfectly.

sole The fleshy inner section of a goat's hoof. It is like an incredibly thick callus and is surrounded by the hoof wall.

stanchion The portion of a milking stand that locks a goat's head in position.

teat tape Paper surgical tape that is strategically placed on a goat's teats to prevent her kids from nursing.

ultrapasteurized A form of pasteurization in which the milk is run through pipes and almost instantaneously heated to approximately 280 degrees F. It improves the shelf life of milk but prevents the milk from being made into cheese.

wall The outer section of a goat's hoof, similar to a fingernail.

wether A neutered male goat.

withers The part of a goat where the shoulders meet the spine.

GOATY RESOURCES

REFERENCES

Brown, Frederick. "Cows in the Commons, Dogs on the Lawn: A History of Animals in Seattle." (PhD diss., University of Washington, 2010).

Daovy, Kongmanila, T. R. Preston, and Inger Ledin. "Selective Behaviour of Goats Offered Different Tropical Foliages," supplement, *Livestock Research for Rural Development* 20 (May 2008).

Dewey, Ariane, and Mitchell Sharmat. *Gregory, the Terrible Eater.* New York: Scholastic, 2009.

Dhiman, T. R., G. R. Anand, L. D. Satter, and M. W. Pariza. "Conjugated Linoleic Acid Content of Milk from Cows Fed Different Diets." *Journal of Dairy Science* 82 (1999): 2146-56.

Domingue, B. M., D. W. Dellow, and T. N. Barry. "The Efficiency of Chewing During Eating and Ruminating in Goats and Sheep." *British Journal of Nutrition* 65 (1991): 355-63.

Eggert, J. M., M. A. Belury, A. Kempa-Steczko, S. E. Mills, and A. P. Schinckel. "Effects of Conjugated Linoleic Acid on the Belly Firmness and Fatty Acid Composition of Genetically Lean Pigs." *Journal of Animal Science* 79 (2001): 2866-72.

Grier, Katherine. *Pets in America: A History.* Chapel Hill: University of North Carolina Press, 2006.

Mendelson, Anne. *Milk: The Surprising Story of Milk Through the Ages.* New York: Alfred A. Knopf, 2008.

Pollan, Michael. *The Omnivore's Dilemma.* New York: Penguin, 2007.

Simopoulos, Artemis P., and Jo Robinson. *The Omega Diet.* New York: Harper, 1999.

Smith, Cheryl. *Goat Health Care,* Cheshire, OR: Karmadillo Press, 2009.

GOAT EQUIPMENT CATALOGS

Caprine Supply, www.caprinesupply.com, 1-800-646-7736

Hoegger Supply, www.hoeggerfarmyard.com, 1-800-221-4628

Quality Llama Products, Inc. and Alternate Livestock Supply, www.llamaproducts.com. Supplies halters, bridles, goat carts.

Bun-Bag, www.bunbag.com. For bun/berry bags.

GOAT KEEPING BOOKS

Get Your Goat: How to Keep Happy, Healthy Goats in Your Backyard, Wherever You Live, by Brent Zimmerman. Minneapolis, MN: Quarry Books, 2012.
This book has an extremely helpful section on kidding and repositioning kids stuck in the birth canal.

Raising Goats for Dummies, by Cheryl K. Smith. Hoboken, NJ: Wiley, 2010.
This is an all-around helpful guide to raising goats.

Goat Health Care, by Cheryl K. Smith. Cheshire, OR: Karmadillo Press, 2009.
This book has lots of helpful information on a wide variety of goat diseases.

GOAT CARE WEBSITES

GoatWisdom: www.goatwisdom.com

Fias Co Farm: www.fiascofarm.com

Jack & Anita Mauldin Boer Goats: www.jackmauldin.com

EXTENSION SERVICES NATIONWIDE

The U.S. Department of Agriculture provides a list of all of the extension services within the United States at www.csrees.usda.gov /Extension

CHEESE-MAKING BOOKS AND WEBSITES

Goats Produce Too! The Udder Real Thing, Volume II, by Mary Jane Toth (self-published), 1989.

Home Cheese Making, by Ricki Carroll. North Adams, MA: Storey Publishing, 2002.

Homemade Cheese—Recipes for 50 Cheeses from Artisan Cheesemakers, by Janet Hurst. Minneapolis, MN: Voyageur Press, 2011.

Artisan Cheese Making at Home, by Mary Karlin. New York: Ten Speed Press, 2011. Also the accompanying website: www.artisancheesemakingathome.com

Beginning Cheese Making website by David Fankhauser: http://biology.clc.uc.edu/ fankhauser/cheese/cheese.html

MILKING STAND DIRECTIONS

The Prairie Homestead: www.theprairiehomestead.com/2011/04 /building-a-goat-milking-stand.html

Fias Co Farm: www.fiascofarm.com/goats/milkstand.html

Melissa Thomas in *Dairy Goat Journal:* www.dairygoatjournal.com/issues/85/85-3 /Melissa_Thomas.html

The Goat Spot: http://thegoatspot.net

GOAT PACKING SUPPLIES AND TRAIL INFORMATION

Northwest Pack Goats: http://northwestpackgoats.com

Edelweiss Acres: http://home.comcast.net/~edelweissacres

Butt-Head Pack Goats:
www.buttheadpackgoats.com

Horse & Mule Trail Guide USA:
www.horseandmuletrails.com

Horse Trails and Campgrounds:
www.horsetraildirectory.com

HOOF TRIMMING INFORMATION

Basic Hoof Trimming DVD, by Northwest Pack
Goats. Available through their website at
http://northwestpackgoats.com

Goat Hoof Trimming page on
International Kiko Goat Association website:
http://theikga.org/hoof_trimming.html

DIAGNOSTIC LABS

BioTracking, www.biotracking.com.
Also known as bioPRYN, this company
provides Caprine Arthritis and Encephalitis
(CAE) and pregnancy testing for goats.

CLICKER TRAINING

Getting Started: Clicker Training for Dogs,
by Karen Pryor. Waltham, MA: Sunshine Books,
2002. Also the accompanying website,
www.clickertraining.com

The Power of Positive Dog Training, by Pat Miller.
Hoboken, NJ: Wiley: Howell Book House, 2001.

POSTSCRIPT

A FEW YEARS BACK, I HEADED OUT OF TOWN with my son and pug dog to the annual Pug Gala held at the Evergreen State Fairgrounds in Monroe. As the event drew to a close and the pugs began to droop and head out to their cars to nap on their rides home, Spencer and I stood in the parking lot and noticed an odd assortment of antique washing machines and tractors and a building with a sign out front that said, "museum." We stepped inside and, being the only ones around, got a private tour. There was an old cream separator, a wood-powered kitchen stove, a rope-making machine, and a pre-electrical refrigeration machine that used creek water flowing through copper pipes to cool milk down to 40 degrees F in a matter of minutes. When the curator learned that I was interested specifically in the history of farm animals in cities, he went into a back room and returned with an old, stylish lavender hatbox. When he worked the lid of the hatbox up and off, I saw within a tattered and yellowed manuscript. What I learned from reading through it that afternoon intrigued me.

Although many people are unaware of this, F. Scott Fitzgerald was one of America's earliest proponents of goat legalization. In the 1920s, a dark period in American history for farm animals, Fitzgerald watched in pained dismay as city codes in urban areas across the United States were revised to oust cows, horses, ducks, chickens, and goats from the city limits.

As a lover of cows and especially goats, F. Scott took this ousting hard. In fact, he took it so hard that he began to drink heavily. He also began to feel a need to write about it and soon was driven to write what many consider his best work, the American classic *The Great Gatsby*. In his original manuscript, a bootlegger and goat enthusiast named Jay

Gatz keeps several goats, and his favorite is named Myrtle. Jay gives Myrtle to Daisy, a married woman he'd met in his youth and admired ever since. Daisy can't get over what a great goat Myrtle is. Tom, Daisy's husband, gets upset because he thinks Jay's gift of Myrtle is part of a scheme to seduce Daisy and steal her away. In this, Tom is right.

While Tom is seething about what he feels is the inappropriate gift of a goat, he is also mad at goats in general because he is a real estate developer and goats are getting in the way of his business dealings. On the day his wife Daisy receives the goat Myrtle, a goat farmer in Long Island refuses Tom's offer to buy his land, which for years has housed his herd of prize-winning Swiss Alpine goats. This refusal to sell messes up one of Tom's biggest, albeit also very shady, real estate schemes. One afternoon, just after meeting with the goat farmer who is still stubbornly refusing to sell him the goat farmland, Tom comes home to find Myrtle the goat eating daisies on his front lawn. He's a man with anger problems and has built up a lot of goat-directed rage. In addition, he is lacking in moral fiber, so when he sees the goat eating his daisies, he runs her down with his car and then backs over her. Not satisfied with murdering a single goat, he drives off and runs over the goat farmer who won't sell the land, as well as Jay, the goat-loving bootlegger. Tom then tells Daisy that they had better skip town and head to their home in the Bahamas.

Daisy is happy to skip town. She is feeling guilty because it turns out that she hasn't been washing Myrtle's udder properly and, as a result, Myrtle has contracted mastitis. This helps explains why Myrtle didn't get out of Tom's way when she saw him gunning for her with the car. She had not been feeling her best and wasn't as alert as usual. In the end, Tom and Daisy drive off and Jay Gatz is left with two broken legs and the sense that Daisy is an irresponsible goat owner and a poor choice for a girlfriend. In this original version of the book, Jay Gatz moves to Montana to heal and be with goats in a rural area where goat-hating real estate agents are scarce.

You may find this hard to believe and ask, "How did the plot get changed around so much?" What happened is that Maxwell Perkins, a closet goat hater and Fitzgerald's editor, knew about F. Scott's drinking problem and revised the manuscript according to the whims of his third wife, also a goat hater. When asked to approve the final version of the story, F. Scott was three sheets to the wind and signed off on the changes. Had he not done so, *The Great Gatsby* would stand today, not just as a great novel but also as one that changed history. As Upton Sinclair's *The Jungle* is remembered for instigating the enactment of today's food safety regulations, and as Harriet Beecher Stowe's *Uncle Tom's Cabin* is remembered for fueling the Civil War, *The Great Gatsby* would be remembered as helping to end the banning of farm animals from cities.

Although Perkins significantly altered the plot line of *The Great Gatsby*, much of the language of the novel survived intact. Such is the case with the last line of the novel, which, according to the original manuscript read, "And so we beat on, goats against the current, borne back ceaselessly into the past."

What exactly is Fitzgerald saying here? This is a question that scholars have debated for many years. I think it's clear that in this great last line, he is lamenting the loss of goats from our day-to-day lives. He points to how, in our modern goat-hating era, we are beaten down by our culture of consumption. Jay, having had his favorite goat run down, must retreat to earlier times, times he finds in the quiet fields of the Montana landscape.

Fitzgerald's last sentence rings as true today as it did when he first penned it. While legalizing goats may be hard work, we must beat on against the current of the antigoat coalition to bring goats back into our modern world. Goats, with their strange rectangular eyes and stubborn, curious personalities, can help us combat the emptiness of our material age.

Great literature often offers great lessons. Such is the case with the long-lost *Great Gatsby* manuscript. Through allegory, it points out that while keeping goats in urban or, in the case of Long Island, suburban settings, is a lot of work, it is also what can help bring meaning to our lives through love, good food, adventure, and friendship.

INDEX

Mary Cruse enjoys her dog and calf on the front porch of her Bellevue home circa 1920, just as the concept of farm animals and pets being one and the same began to vanish from the American psyche. Author Jennie Grant believes it's time to reclaim Mary's viewpoint. *(Photo courtesy Eastside Heritage Center)*

CHARITY LYNN

Author Jennie Grant is a stay-at-home mother in Seattle who has become known locally as the founder and president of the Goat Justice League, a citizen action group that worked with the Seattle City Council to legalize keeping goats in the city in 2007. Grant also teaches backyard goat keeping at Seattle Tilth and has been profiled in *The Seattle Times* as well as in the *New York Times* and on *The Splendid Table*.

Harley Soltes is a photojournalist with a deep appreciation of farming and farmers. Working as a staff photographer for *The Seattle Times* for over twenty years he has shot world events, celebrities, sports, fashion, and everyday life. His work has been published in the *New York Times, Sports Illustrated, Time, Life,* and *Natural Geographic.* He resides on an organic farm in Bow, Washington. See more of his work at www .harleysoltes.com.

OTHER TITLES FROM SKIPSTONE

THE URBAN FARM HANDBOOK
City-Slicker Resources for Growing, Raising, Sourcing, Trading and Preparing What You Eat
Annette Cottrell and Joshua McNichols
Photography by Harley Soltes
You don't have to live on 50 acres to begin
taking control over what you eat

CHEFS ON THE FARM
Recipes and Inspiration from the Quillisascut Farm School of the Domestic Arts
Shannon Borg, Lora Lee Misterly and Karen Jurgensen
Photography by Harley Soltes
A visually rich tour of an organic farm, where award-
winning chefs learn sustainable food practices

UNCLE DAVE'S COW
And Other Whole Animals My Freezer Has Known
Leslie Miller
A guide to sourcing, storing, and preparing
healthy, locally raised meat

FOOD GROWN RIGHT, IN YOUR BACKYARD
A Beginner's Guide to Growing Crops at Home
Colin McCrate and Brad Halm
Photography by Hilary Dahl
Easy gardening instruction for saving money and
eating better by growing your own food in the city

URBAN PANTRY
Tips and Recipes for a Thrifty, Sustainable & Seasonal Kitchen
Amy Pennington
A modern, sustainable approach for stocking
an efficient kitchen

SKIPSTONE

www.skipstonebooks.org
www.mountaineersbooks.org
800-553-4453